"I Sense You"

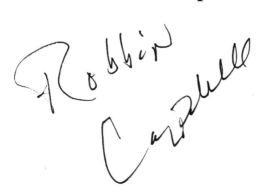

To Elisabeth
a great friend
Enjoy our friendship

Robbin Campbell

Robbin
Campbell

First published by Dog Ear Publishing
4010 W. 86th Street, Ste H
Indianapolis, IN 46268
www.dogearpublishing.net

ISBN: 978-1-4575-2104-1

This book is printed on acid-free paper.

Printed in the United States of America

This book is dedicated to my family, whom I love deeply, and to my friends at work who really helped me to hone my gift and who offered themselves to help me feel more comfortable with it. I would not be where I am today without them. I would like to send out special blessings to my grandma Delpha Allen and my great-great-grandma Mindy Briggs, whom I received my gifts from. And of course, thanks and blessings go to my spirit guides and angels who helped me with my readings with doing Reiki, and with making the right decisions in my life.

Lastly, it is dedicated to my husband, Surachart, who put up with me, while I was obsessing about finishing this book.

Buddha Bless

Preface

My book is titled, *"I Sense You"*, because I have the ability of clairsentience, which means I am able to sense things about people. I have long been able to sense things about family and friends but have not really felt comfortable enough to tell them, until now.

The purpose of this book is to let all sensitive's know that there are a lot of us. Some of you may be just coming into your gift and may feel alienated by what some people say. I hope my book will show you how I also struggled and how I persevered, once I made a conscious decision to embrace my ability. I realize that some of what you read here may scare you, but through time, I had to learn accept it as part of who I am.

CONTENTS

My Gift

We can go through our lives hiding many secrets, then the time arrives to come clean. I am coming clean about my gift, that I am a sensitive and most of my family has no idea exactly what I am able to do. Some of them know about what I have written in chapters such as: "The Yellow Veil over My Crib," "Okay, Mom, It's Time to Cross Over," "Daddy and the Long Road Home," and "Harold's 40- Year Visitation," but most don't. After they've read this book, I hope they will be able to better understand why I used to say the things I said and act the way I did.

As a sensitive, my body reacts differently than other people's bodies to certain situations. Even when doing something or going somewhere makes me uncomfortable, I would do it anyway to keep the peace. Before my mom died, she told me that she admired that most about me, that I never deliberately did or said anything to hurt someone's feelings and always tried to keep the peace within the family, got along with everybody, never picked sides. Honestly, I never realized that I was doing all this, because it was in my nature. It wasn't in me to be confrontational. Actually, I felt people who were constantly like that were just very unhappy with their lives so they lashed out at others to try to show their own superiority. Being naïve, I assumed that once those people grew up, they would realize how immature their actions were. A hard lesson for me to learn was that some adults never do grow up.

As I got older, however, I began to change. I became more confident in myself and made the decision not to really care anymore about hurting certain people's feelings. Why? Because some-times, people need to be told when what they are saying is hurtful or disrespectful. Of course, I always did it in a kind way. This would make them feel even worse, because I was able to do it without ranting and raving like an idiot.

Once I turned 50, my senses went into overdrive. Things that didn't bother me before, do now. I work at the mall, yet I prefer to shop in smaller stores.Huge gatherings of people cause me to experience anxiety, sometimes. Reading in front of a crowd and talking affects me by causing extreme nervousness, eventhough I love to talk. I guess it depends on the energy people are giving off. Out of all the things that I dislike that cause me anxiety and being nervous, I most dread driving on the highway. Whenever I am driving on the highway, I am overwhelmed by the other drivers' total disregard for the safety of human life and about how dangerous the two-ton machines they are driving are-especially those drivers who run up on you trying to get you to get out of their way because they think they own the road and you shouldn't be out there, because you are going only five miles over the speed limit. And let's not forget about the extremely careless ones who are talking or texting on their phones while their cars slowly cross into your lane or, finally, the young men who you can barely see, because their seats are laid back so far. The first time I saw one of these young men, I literally thought the car was driving itself. My heart can't take much more of this.

No, I don't know everything that is going to happen, and I hate it when people say that. What I do get comes from the guidance of my angels and spirit guides, whom I give all the thanks to. I have come to love and cherish my gift, and I know that I am to use it only for good.

CHAPTER 1

The Yellow Veil over My Crib

I was born on February 15, 1959, at Kate Bitting Reynolds Hospital. Back then, new mothers stayed in the hospital one week; now they rush you out in 48 hours or less. Well, during the week my mom and I were there, my dad's mom, Delpha Allen, died, on February 19. She had been very sick and didn't have the opportunity to see me before she passed. My dad was in the armed services, so he was allowed to come home for her funeral, then he had to go back. Mom had plenty of help at home, though: all my sisters; my aunt Thelma; and her mom, Grandma McCoy. Mom said I was a pretty good baby, slept well, didn't cry too much, not too fussy. But one night a week after Grandma Allen died, I was the opposite: crying, acting fussy, because I was hungry.

The house was dark, so Mom felt her way to the kitchen to heat me a bottle. As she approached the dark kitchen, she thought she saw someone sitting in the chair by the door. The bathroom light was on, but the door was almost completely closed except for a small beam of light that showed through. It kind of scared her, so she pushed open the bathroom door and saw that nobody was in the chair. She flipped on the kitchen light and thought, *I must really be tired because I'm seeing things,* as she heated my bottle. In case you don't know, in-1959, heating a bottle meant putting it in water that was boiling on the stove. Were microwaves, even made back then?

Okay, lets get back to the story. Mom headed back to the room, and as she entered the room, she noticed a faint yellow veil over my crib. It stopped her in her tracks when she realized that I was actually reaching for this veil as it hovered over my tiny body. Mom turned on the light, and poof!, the veil was gone. She picked me up to make sure that I was okay.

Needless to say, she was more than a little unnerved by both of these incidents. I was fed my bottle and went right back to sleep. Mom told Dad what had happened and his reply was that it was probably his mom, my Grandma Allen, finally getting the chance to see her grandbaby.

Grandma Delpha Allen had been buried in yellow and had had the sense of sight; I feel she passed it on to me. I can't prove it, but I think a few of my sisters have some abilities also. I have always sensed it.I bet back then, all people with abilities struggled with trying to keep them secret. No one talked about it, because it was considered taboo or witchcraft. But thank you, Delpha Allen, for giving birth to John Henry Allen, and thanks to him for marrying Eulalia Elizabeth McCoy, and let's not forget John Lucious McCoy and Mary Tindal McCoy for having Eulalia. Without all of you, I wouldn't be the special person I am today.

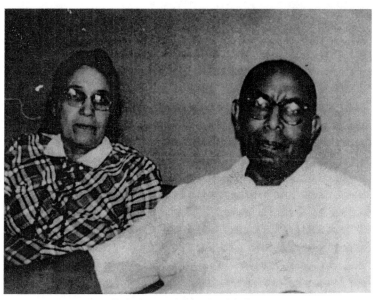

Grandma and Grandpa McCoy

CHAPTER 2

My First

My earliest recollection of my special gift was when I was around six years old. Grandpa Popeye McCoy had passed away. Everyone called him Popeye because he had big bulging eyes, I guess. He was a cigar smoker and a heavy drinker, and he could throw out a few cuss words, from what I can remember. Grandpa had had a stroke and was in a wheelchair. I don't really recall seeing him any other way, and I don't know how long he had been in that wheelchair before he died. He gave off an aire of being a hard man, but he was always very kind and funny to me; that's why I liked being with him and Grandma McCoy.

For some reason, I have always enjoyed the company of old people. Grandpa and Grandma fascinated me with all their stories of how they had grown up and all the chores they'd had to do before and after school. Kids now-a-days would never survive such chores; most are too busy lying around watching TV or on the Internet.

A few days after we had buried Grandpa McCoy, I spent the night over at their house. I can still remember how soft and pillowy the bed was. Now-a-days, if I slept in a bed that soft, I wouldn't be able to move the next morning because my back would be killing me. As I slept that night, I had my first dream about a deceased person, Grandpa Popeye. In my dream, he was in a uniform and was walking. Now, remember I had never seen him or didn't recall seeing him in any way except in that wheelchair, so I asked him how he was able to walk, and he said that when people pass on, they are able to take on the form of the happiest time in their life if they choose, and he had been proudest when he'd served in the military.

He took my hand, and we started walking and talking. Then somehow, we ended up back at the house. We sat down on the couch, and he told me what he wanted me to go back and tell Mary (my grandma). He talked about the coins under the bed, which she already knew about, then he told me about some other papers and where to tell her to find them. Grandpa hugged me, and I cried because I didn't want him to leave, but he said his mission was complete and he needed to crossover. At that time, I didn't know what crossing over meant. Did he have to cross over the street or a river? Cross over what? Then he was gone forever. I have never dreamt of him again.

In the morning, I jumped out of bed and told Grandma everything Grandpa had said. She told me that it was not nice to say things like that about the dead and that I needed to keep things like that to myself or some people might think I was crazy. I was crushed; I wasn't lying. I really had talked to him. She called up my mom and told her what I had said (I was eavesdropping, that's how I know.) She asked Mom if Mom had told me about the coins under the bed in the room where Grandpa Popeye had slept (no, Mom hadn't), and she asked Mom what papers I was talking about. Later, my mom sat me down and told me to be very careful about saying things like that to people because they would think I was talking nonsense.

After that, I spent a lot of time with my Grandma McCoy. I went to work with her sometimes, but we never talked about that dream again. I really liked spending the night over at her house, and through the years, a lot of my dreams were focused around or in her house. Probably because I felt it was a safe haven and I felt so comfortable there.

Thank you, Grandpa. I salute you, for being my first communication with the spirit world.

CHAPTER 3

Kinship with the Old

When I was just a few years old, I became very attached to one of my mom's friends, Mrs. Viola Blair. She had lost her son many years before, and I saw her and her husband as being two really nice old people. Her husband, Mr. Blair, drove a big old red truck that he hauled junk and wood around in. He never said much, but he would give me a smile every once in a while. Mrs. Viola was different, though; she was the sweetest, kindest person you would ever want to meet. I was told that I had run to Mrs. Viola when my mom had brought home my brother Harold from the hospital. Wow, showing signs of jealousy at barely two years old. I don't know about other people, but I really can't remember a lot about my childhood before the age of five. *I do remember* times spent with Mrs. Viola, though, and of course the trauma of getting my finger busted by a lunatic at Cleveland Avenue Pre-school, because he liked me. This toxic person made my pre-school days a living hell and continued to go to school with me through to junior high school.

Mrs. Viola's house was small and clean. Mr. Blair had built on a extra room in the back of the house. This was where she kept all of her dolls. Through the years, I would go up to her house (two houses from mine) after school, go to the store to get her a can of snuff and me some candy, and then play with her beautiful porcelain dolls. I know it was strange, but I have always liked spending time with old people, as I mentioned earlier, listening to them tell me how things had been when they were young. They taught me to appreciate all the freedoms we had in our time.

Sometimes when I was playing at Mr. and Mrs. Blair's house, I would go by the bedroom and see a man lying on the bed. Whenever I told Mrs. Viola, she said her son was very sick and I should just let him rest. I was seven or eight, maybe, but I knew that her son was dead, because people in the neighborhood talked about it. She probably thought I had a vivid imagination and was just being nice by acknowledging that I saw him there. Why is it that really nice people either can't have children or they lose a child and that people who don't deserve to have children or don't even want to take care of the ones they have, just keep spitting them out? I was thinking that at a very young age, and it still seems to hold true now. I always wondered if Mrs. Viola's wanting a child so bad was why her son kept hanging around the house. After, seeing Grandpa Popeye in my dream, I understood that some spirits would stay here on earth with us until their missions were complete. I now wonder how long Mrs. Viola's son had been there, because I had never noticed him until after my experience with my own grandpa.

I continued to visit Mrs. Viola throughout my teenage years, and even when I became pregnant, got married, and had my son, Priest, by my 16th birthday, she remained a very special part of my life. God put me in her life, and it was my mission at that time to stay in her life. I ended up being the child she no longer had in her life. I also made her a godparent to my son.

During the next several years, Mrs. Viola Blair's health started to fail and poor Mr. Blair passed. I worried about Mrs. Viola being all by herself. In all the years I had spent at her home, her only family I had known of was her sister who lived around the corner off 21st Street. Her sister was a very sweet person, too.

In April 1983, I was pregnant with my second child. By August, I had terrible morning sickness. Why the hell do they call it morning sickness when you have it in the afternoon and at night? I had lost 15 pounds and had been in the hospital for dehydration, so when Mrs. Viola fell really ill and had to be put in the hospital herself, I was too sick to go see her. I finally pulled myself together long enough to go see her on August 8, but by that time, she didn't even know who I was. I sat in my car outside of the hospital and cried, asking, "God, why would you let this happen? I know that you put me in her life for a reason. My God, I was sick. Why would you let her not know me when I was finally able to get over there to see her?" Of course, I never got an answer. After being mad at God for quite a while, I learned that I needed to be thankful for the time that I had been given with her and I knew that I had brought a lot of joy to her and Mr. Blair's hearts.

On August 10, Mrs. Viola passed at Forsyth Memorial Hospital. She was buried on August 13. She had been a member of New Bethel Baptist Church, where she had served on the Spiritual Choir, Missionary Circle#3, the Nurses Board, Effort Club, Ladies Aid, and Sunday School Class#2. Viola Spencer Blair had also been a member of the 17th Street Goodwill Community Club with my mom. My daughter, Pilar, was born five months later, in January 1984, and I know Mrs. Viola got to see her.

From the age of 6 to the age of 25, I had seen a lot of death, including my grandpa and my father, John Henry, in 1977. My dad had suffered with cancer for so long that I prayed to God not to continue to let him suffer, yet when he did finally die, I felt like someone had put their hand on my heart and squeezed it so hard that I couldn't breathe. His death, I felt, took a part of me, and it took me a long time to get that part back, to make myself feel whole again. My dad and my grandfather both came to me in my dreams to help me be able to accept their passing, but Mrs. Viola has never come to me. This really bothered me about my gift, why would I not be able to see all the people I love when they pass on but be able to know things about total strangers? This confusion about my abilities is why I feel that I tried to suppress them from my late teens through my mid-thirties.

Surachart and Robbin's wedding on September 14, 1974.

Surachart, Priest and Robbin standing outside Mrs. Hairston's house.

CHAPTER 4

Baby in Pink

Throughout high school, I had many friends and, I'm sure, some enemies, but thankfully, I never got into any fights. Actually, my years in school were pretty normal. I had several best friends, and sometimes, I would spend time over at their houses and sometimes they would come to visit me at my house. I remember when we were in middle school playing games and of course talking about boys. In the early 70's, my neighborhood was so safe that we would lie down in the grass and look up at the clear beautiful night sky and try to count the stars or point out the constellations, not a worry in the world. As we got older, we fell in love with Elvis and his song "Rubbernecking." We played it all the time and danced in the yard. We talked about kissing boys and if it would lead to getting pregnant. I can't remember who told us that, and I also can't quite recall which one of us first proved that theory was wrong.

Does anybody remember the game "cars"? You know, the car that comes up or down the street, during your turn, it was yours. If it was cool, you were okay, but if it was old or torn up, you were laughed at. We loved that game, and that is actually how I met my husband. He and 3 of his friends were riding down the street and they stopped and asked if we knew this guy who lived down the street. I can only imagine some of you are saying, that is so lame, compared to what kids do for fun now, but when I came up we spent time playing games outside and having fun being out in the sunshine. We didn't stay inside all day playing on a computer or with video games, which for me is probably good, because my brain tends to not be able to calm down when I am around too many electronics.

A lot of times when I was walking the halls at school, I would sense stuff about people, but I kept it to myself. After years of being told to stop saying what I had seen or what some spirit had told me. I began to realize that maybe this wasn't always such a great gift, and I had to work harder to ignore it. Sometimes this was very hard, like when my brother Harold died in Butner, North Carolina. When he was a baby, he had fallen out of a chair and it had caused brain damage. Mom and Dad had kept him at home as long as they could. My siblings and I would help to take care of him, but Mom was still having babies, and as Harold got older, his behavior became more erratic. Back then, the Murdoch Center at Butner was where you sent children who were mentally challenged, had behavioral problems, or were autistic. We would visit him every other weekend. My dad was one of those heavy-footed drivers who sometimes had fits of road rage and would say things such as, "What the xxxx is wrong with that stupid xxx. Those trips were very special, and my siblings and I loved hearing my dad say stuff like that, because we would laugh our heads off and Momma would say, "Johnny! Now, is all that necessary?" That was my dad; I loved him no matter what. I guess that's why I married a man with the same mouth, who graciously passed it down to my son. Oh well, memories.

Anyway, Harold died from an allergic reaction to some medicine that he had been given. The family had visited him the weekend before and noticed that he had a rash. My dad and mom had questioned it and been told that Harold was being given an antibiotic to clear it up.

When we learned that Harold had died, I had to leave the house and go outside because I was becoming overwhelmed with their grief. I didn't really cry until the funeral; I don't know why. I knew Harold was in a better place, but before the funeral was not the time to talk about that, because it was disrespecting the dead as I was always told.

After Harold's funeral, my senses went wild when I walked into the school, and I started having dreams about a baby girl dying. I was also having other crazy dreams, but the one that bothered me most was of the dead baby girl dressed in pink. She was so beautiful, lying in her small casket, as everyone in her family stood around crying. I would wake up crying, myself. I asked the angels to please stop making me have this dream and asked what the angels were trying to tell or show me. I kept having the dream and I didn't have anyone to talk to about it.

I feel that my dad would have understood what I was going through, but he was always working and so busy, plus he had started having problems with his hand. I knew it was something bad but didn't know it would end up being cancer. The dreams continued, and then one of my friends had a miscarriage. I went to the funeral home to show my respect, and I stepped into déjà vue. It was a scene from my dream. The baby in the casket was a dark-skinned little girl, dressed in pink. I just stood at the casket. I was at a loss for words. As I walked home, I asked God and all his angels to take special care of her. She deserved that, because had she survived, she would have had a great mommy.

John Henry and Eulalia McCoy Allen (Robbin's parents)

CHAPTER 5

Daddy and the Long Road Home

When I was growing up, my dad had so many jobs, we rarely got the chance to see or talk to him. He worked fulltime at the hospital in Salisbury, so he drove from Winston to Salisbury daily. He also had a part-time job as a security guard at the post office. Dad was a Shriner and had reserve duty one weekend out of each month, and on his down time, he was always taking a course in school for something, such as learning to cut hair, upholster furniture and who knows what else.

Being raised by a single mother, he had had instilled in him a very strong work ethic. My grandma Allen was a sensitive, and I feel that's who I got my ability from. She would tell Daddy whether or not he should be doing something. One particular night, he and three of his friends wanted to go out partying and drinking. When his mom found out, she asked him not to go because she had had a vision of an accident with a tree. Grandma was adamant about something bad happening. Dad tried to warn his friends by telling them what his mom had seen, but they laughed it off, and my dad watched them drive away. A few hours after midnight, someone came knocking at the door to tell Daddy that there had been a really bad accident. Evidently, his three friends had gone drinking and tried to drive home. They had been going too fast for a curve, and the car had flown off the road and wrapped around a tree. They had all been killed instantly.

Getting back to the long road home, Dad was driving home from Salisbury late one night when he came upon a girl lying in the road. She was hurt, so he stopped to help her. He picked her up and laid her in the back seat of the station wagon. He drove back to the hospital and pulled up to the emergency room. When he opened the back door, she had vanished. He began to ask around about the lady on the highway and was told by several of the nurses that people frequently drove to the emergency room with a young lady who had vanished by the time they got there to drop her off.

The ghost story goes like this: A young lady was the victim of a hit-and-run accident on that stretch of highway where Dad had found her. Her ghost lies along that stretch of highway until a kind stranger stops to pick her up. Dad said this story was true, but, of course, my dad was known to tell some pretty tall tales.

CHAPTER 6

An Unblessed Home

During the summer of 1981, when my son, Priest, was six years old, my husband, Priest and I moved into an old two-story house on Sprague Street in Winston Salem. It was across the street from a church, so I thought it would be a nice peaceful home to live in. There were two bedrooms upstairs and one downstairs. The kitchen and bathroom were small, but the living room and entertainment room were big. The entertainment room had an angled bar; it was the bomb. Every time someone came over, we would end up in that room, listening to music and sipping on gin and juice. My husband, Chart, had bought a huge Brothers Johnson picture, and we had hung it on the wall; it was perfect. I loved to bartend and make mixed drinks, so I would have to say that this room was my favorite. We also had a little black padded bar with flashing lights inside of it. It was the type of bar people had in their home when they couldn't afford an expensive real-looking one. The screen in front of the lights on the bar was cracked and taped together because Priest had been dancing in front of it when we had been in an apartment on 3rd street and had fallen into it. That was our accident-prone son.

In November of that year, my two nieces, Charlene and Charlette, came to live with us for a month or so. This turned out to be great, because Priest would have someone to play with and my nieces were really good babysitters and helpers around the house. During this time, I continued to realize that we were not alone in the house and the entity, spirit, or whatever you want to call it was not nice. Even though I had tried to repress my abilities since we had moved in, and for almost ten years by that time, I was still able to sense danger. It unnerved me to realize that what I was dealing with was something evil and sinister. I hate to say it, but the entity was very strong and able to control how I felt. I had an almost uncontrollable desire to have sex. Whenever I took a bath or shower, I could feel someone's hands caressing me, then I would snap out of it and feel as if I had been in a trance. Several times when I was in the house by myself, I would end up in bed and feel the presence. What was happening really started to freak me out. Then Priest started being afraid to sleep in his room, so I moved my nieces upstairs with him.

One evening while Chart was still at work and the kids were watching TV upstairs, I decided to make lunches for the next day. I was in the kitchen when all of a sudden, the kids started hollering my name. After dropping the knife on the floor, I ran upstairs as fast as I could. They were trying to tell me that the gray chair downstairs in the bedroom/den was rocking back and forth on its own. They had seen it through a vent in the floor that allowed them to see into the bedroom/den. I refused to believe what they had to say, even though I knew that there was something in the home. I guess I thought if we didn't acknowledge the presence, it would leave. As I walked back downstairs, I went past the room. Then I doubled back and looked to see if the chair was still rocking. It wasn't.

Charlene, Charlette, and Priest were obsessed with staring down that vent to see if the chair was going to move again. Sure enough, about an hour later, it happened again. They screamed my name, and I ran past the den without even looking. Getting to the kids was the only thing on my mind. Once I got upstairs, I could tell that they were scared and upset, so I got down on my knees and peered through the vent. The gray chair was rocking back and forth. Now I was shaking, but I was the adult, so I needed to keep it together. We hovered around each other and started toward the stairs. Remember, this was an old home, so it creaked a lot. The kids hollered with each step, and this made my heart beat even faster. By the time we got to the bottom of the stairs, we were all nervous wrecks and after looking in the den that damn chair had stopped rocking. I yelled, "Get out of my house." I don't want you here; you are not welcome. Leave now! That night, I slept in Priest's room with the kids until Chart got home. The next day I called off of work at Davis Department Store, I was a total mess. I pleaded with my husband to find us another place to live. He knew that the kids and I were upset about the chair rocking on its own, but that was all he knew. Being embarrassed about the other part, the uncontrollable desire to have sex and feeling the presence there, when I would end up on the bed. I couldn't bring myself to mention that or the shadows that I had been seeing.

The kids wanted to get the heck out of Dodge, so they ran out the door to go to school. I don't think Chart believed us, but he was concerned. After he left for work, I went next door to talk to my neighbors. They were two sisters, around 60 years old, and they wondered why it had taken me so long to come over and talk with them. They had a lot to say. It seemed that no family who had moved into that house ever stayed there very long. The previous family had been a preacher and his wife and children, who had left in the middle of the night. "Honey," they told me, "you need a blessing, cause you live in an unblessed home."

After leaving the sister's house, I went across the street to the church and asked the pastor to come and bless the home. I had to plead for his help. He came over and did a blessing. While in the house, he said that there was a bad spirit in it. No shit. When he left, the house did feel lighter, at least for a few weeks, then it started back up. Luckily, by this time, we had found a townhouse. My nieces went back home, and my family moved out, never to return. Many years later, we drove past the place and found that it had been remodeled and turned into four rental rooms for students. I have always wondered if the remodel made the haunting worse.

Priest, Charlette and Charlene outside of the "Unblessed Home"

My sister Yvonne and brother John in the entertainment room
inside the "Unblessed Home"

CHAPTER 7

The Ghost in the Shoe Department

I n February of 1995, I started as the manager of the ladies' and men's shoe departments at Belk. They were both very busy areas, so it kept me running from the ladies' department on level two to the men's department on level one. The ladies' shoe area put-backs always got backed up, and a lot of times, the girls who worked there were not able to get those shoes put away until the next day, so I started coming in at 7a.m. to set up all the tables for advertised items so when the girls got in, they could focus on getting all the shoes put away. This also made it easier for the stockperson to get new shoes into the stockroom shelves. The first four or five times I came in early, everything was quiet, but one morning not long after, I had decided to work on some paperwork in my office, which happened to be on the top level of the ladies shoe stockroom. Something was not quite right that morning. I kept getting an uneasy feeling, as if someone was watching me. Then I saw a shadow go by. *Okay, Robbin, I know it's quiet and kind of spooky*, I told myself. *Get yourself together. You know the mind can play tricks on you.* So I sat back down and continued working. *Oh hell, now I can actually sense somebody looking at me.* I turned my head, and there he was, peering through the shelf, and he stayed there long enough for me to see him. Then he disappeared. *No, No, No! I am not see-*

ing a ghost, **I thought.** My heart was racing in my chest, but I had to go see if there was anything really there.

"Hello, is anybody up here? Hello," I called. I felt like one of those stupid people in a horror movie, where they are walking through a house and asking if anybody is there when they should start running and get out of the path of some psychotic killer or lunatic ghost. Call me stupid (it won't be the last time I do something like this), because I was doing just that. After looking around, I decided to stay downstairs until the stock girl came in at 8a.m. When she finally arrived, I helped her to put stock out, to keep my mind off what had just happened, and I stopped coming in early.

The next week, I decided to take another chance, and I started coming in at 7a.m. again. Nothing happened, so I stopped thinking about it. I have always enjoyed peace and quiet, and coming in early, I was able to get much more work done. Coming in early, I planned what shoes will go on which tables, put any extras under the skirted table, and had it all complete by store opening.

Between helping to keep the tables straight and filled in, waiting on customers, and helping in the stockroom, I was always falling behind on my paperwork, so the next morning, after I had started coming back in at 7a.m., I tried to catch up on my reports that had to be turned in by the end of the week. My ghost thought I needed another scare, so this time, he came from out of the wall and walked right past my office and didn't even look my way. He was a young white male, around 25, I sensed and was wearing jeans, shirt, and a white hard hat. Because of the way he was dressed, I assumed he had been a laborer. I knew that the third level of the store had been added on; I just didn't know when, because I had never shopped at the mall until I'd got a job there. I loved the downtown area and stores, having grown up shopping with my grandma McCoy at Davis, Anchor, Thalheimers and Mother and Daughters. [My grandma bought me a long light green and white dress for my wedding from Mother and Daughters when I couldn't wear white because I was pregnant with my first child. Honestly, being that young, I didn't want to wear white (but I will at my 40th anniversary).]

Back to the ghost. The morning I'd seen the ghost for the second time, after the 9:45a.m. meeting, I headed to the dock to speak to Art and Bob, who had worked at the store for a while, I felt like they would know if something had happened. After I drilled them for answers, they told me an accident had occurred when Level three was built. Bob wanted to know why I was asking, so I had to tell them what I had seen twice while working in my office. I described the young man, what he was wearing. Then I just blatantly asked if a young man had died during construction and had to tell them about my gift. Art asked, "So you really see these people?" and I replied yes. How else would I be able to tell them how this young man looked and what he was wearing? Art and Bob told me that the workers had done the remodeling during the night so they wouldn't disturb the customers during the day. This young man was shot by a male associate who had been fired and was trying to get back in the store with a weapon. The associate went to prison for the young man's murder.

Now I knew why I was there. The minute I first walked through the doors of that store, my radar had gone off, and it has been active, ever since. I sensed that if the young man came to me, it was my job to find out what he wanted and why he was still here. While doing some research on ghosts/spirits being attached to a place, I realized he was still there because of the violence of his death. Switching over to my detective mode, I spoke with numerous associates who had worked at the store during this time (latter 1980's), and

I kept getting pretty much the same story. All of them said that this young man had worked on the crew that had added Level 3 and that was why he was wearing a hard hat, but no one knew his name. Having no name for the young man was frustrating, and so was having no communication with him. Maybe I was just too inexperienced. Maybe I wasn't going to be able to help him. After a month or so, he stopped appearing to me, but I kept hearing the footsteps, and so did the shoe ladies.

After a little over a year of working at Belk, I was promoted to a larger area on level three. The year was 1996, and I took over the moderate and intimate clothing areas. From time to time, I would go down to level two and talk to people in ladies' shoes to see if they were still having any problems. Manager after manager continued to make comments about hearing noises and seeing shadows on the top floor of the stockroom. Then it all stopped. After another couple of years, I was promoted to an even larger area (better sportswear) back on level two. Boy, was I relieved that everything had calmed down.

Several years later, management decided to remodel the ladies' shoe department and triple the size of the floor space and stockroom. It was huge and beautiful. It spread out all the way around to where the old customer service area had been. That particular side, where the level 2 restrooms are located, was closed off with a door that led into the stockroom. Sadly, the old customer service side was also the exact area where he was shot.

After the remodel, the associates started saying that the young man had come back and they were hearing all sorts of footsteps upstairs. Our associate entrance is on that side, so we had to come down that hallway (where his death happened) to get to the main second floor, and every time I came in, I would sense and sometimes see the young man hovering over that side door. He started getting on my nerves. What did he expect me to do? Well, he won out, and I started researching again. I found out that he wasn't a laborer at all and had never worked for Belk, like we did. He had been a Pinkerton guard (got this information from an associate) and had been hired to watch over the workers at night. That's why he was the one who had confronted the associate trying to get back into the store. For me, the final straw was the day I came in and saw blood coming down the walls (there was no real blood, I feel he made me see this, because of my gift). Now this young man's presence, had been sensed by me and many other associates for almost 15 years, and I had to make the decision to end it. He needed to move on. It bothered me because I had been going through film after film and newspaper after newspaper at the library, trying to find an article on him, something with his name on it, but to no avail. I needed a rest from him, and so did the shoe people.

The new shoe stockroom was like a maze. I am very bad with directions, so I asked my friend, Joanna to go into the stockroom with me for moral support and direction. We headed over to the area where the young man had been shot and where I had seen the blood coming down the wall. I went to the metal shelf behind the door; Joanna stood to my right. I laid my hand on the metal rail, and the story all came pouring out. I saw him on the floor with all the blood. Next, I saw his mother crying over his body. I felt all the pain, sorrow, and compassion that this brave young man had for the man who had killed him. There was no hate in his heart, and he deeply wanted the man to know this. I let go and ran outside and cried, inconsolable at that moment. I needed time by myself to grieve for the young man and his family. Throughout the day, I continued to cry, getting it all out. Finally, I was able to give him the acknowledgement he deserved.

*He came to me a ghost in the dark,
A brave young man who had left his mark.
He completed his duties, right to the end,
A sadder outcome, no one could comprehend.
He died with dignity and held no hate,
A kind young man who deserved a better fate.*

CHAPTER 8

Sensing People Out:
My First Readings at Work

At Belk, I was put on a committee to help raise money for United Way. We were bouncing ideas off each other when, out of no-where, I said, "I can do readings for fun to see how much we can raise." So the very next day, I put up a sign-up sheet for 15-minute time slots for $10 each. Within two days, all the times were filled up. My original plan had been to do readings from 10a.m. to 3p.m. Boy, was I naïve.

An associate from our visual team set up a tent and I brought in my Buddha statue, my Durga (an Indian goddess) statue and a sponge (to absorb negative energy), a purple cloth (my spiritual color) for the table, and incense, and I prayed to my spirit guides to help me give these associates accurate readings. I had also prepared myself by reading up on ways to clear myself and the room after each reading to keep from becoming too drained during the five hours. Purple is my spiritual color because of a dream of an angel I had after my thirty-first birthday in 1990. This angelic being was draped in a purple cloak with gold trim. I was told by this angel that purple would be my spiritual and healing color, to work with. When I am surrounded by purple, it gives me a sense of calmness and well-being.

On the day of the readings, I was a little nervous. I had done cold readings (done in the spur of the moment) before, but I had never charged anyone. My spirit guides had told me they would let me know when to start charging people. The year I did these readings at Belk, all proceeds went to United Way. The year was around 1997 or 1998, and I didn't start charging clients until October 2011. At 9:45a.m., I started doing meditation to relax myself, then exactly at 10:00a.m., my first client came in.

As the day went on, the readings were going great, and several associates were amazed at how accurate I was, but there were some who said that their readings were off (they later came back to tell me that what I had said had actually come true but, it just took a couple of months). I am a sensitive, not a psychic, so what I sense may take days, months, even years to happen, I never really know. All I can say is that I tell people exactly what I see at that time and I won't lie. If you come for a reading, then I assume you want the truth.

The readings I did on that day were done like this: I took my client's right hand, cupped both my hands around it, and closed my eyes and told the associate what I saw. During the hours when I did the readings, I was very thirsty but never got hungry. The associates started leaving and telling others in the store how great I was, then more people were trying to get me to do readings after 3p.m. Then it started getting backed up because people were asking too many questions and ended up staying past their 15 minutes. The hallway was getting crowded because associates were asking everybody who came out how their readings had gone. I felt myself getting overwhelmed because I was not able to clear myself or the room in between each person because they were going over time. This is probably why many psychics serve only one person an hour and charge more if you go over that time.

When I did readings that day, I noticed that people didn't care if someone else was waiting. They wanted to get as much info as they could out of me while they were in that room. It's a natural reaction, so I can't say that I blame them. I would probably be the same way if someone was willing to do a reading for me for $10.When I started feeling what my clients were feeling, hurting where they were hurting, I knew I was in trouble. My knee was hurting, I felt like I had tendonitis in my wrist, I had lower back pain, and, the final kicker, I felt the flood of emotional tears. When the associate caused the flood of tears, I told her she was very sick emotionally and hiding something very bad. She asked if I was faking, then she got up and walked out. She was later terminated.

The spookiest moment came at 6:30p.m., (Yes, I had been doing readings for over eight hours, without eating anything or taking a bathroom break.) By this time, my senses were incredibly heightened and I was ready to fall over from sheer exhaustion. I guess I should tell you that from the beginning of that day, I had felt like someone was in the tent with me. I kept asking everybody if they had been adopted. It was crazy. Then my final client, Andrea, came through the door and asked me if I could please do her reading, because she had been waiting since 4p.m. I believed her and for some reason felt that I was definitely supposed to do her reading. I told Andrea to go out and tell everyone else that her reading would be the last.

When Andrea sat down and I took her right hand, I immediately got a rush of emotions: love, loss, compassion, and how beautiful her blue eyes still were. Like all the others before her, I asked if she was adopted. She said no but her deceased husband was. Then the tears really came flooding out. Now I knew who my special guest had been waiting for all day. He felt so much love for her that words cannot express how I felt being between these two and sensing all the emotions that were coming through. Once I composed myself, I told

Andrea what her husband wanted her to know, about the children and her, how he felt she had done a wonderful job raising the girls. I finally started feeling too heavy to continue, so I asked him to leave, but he wouldn't, so I told him to leave immediately. He finally did, and then both Andrea and I cried. (Sometimes the empath in me makes it hard to read certain people whenever a deceased family member influences the outcome.) Whenever I get too emotional during a reading, I can't go on physically. My spirit guides help me all the time, but other influences affect me being able to do an accurate reading. Andrea's reading was more of a visitation. Sometimes the deceased interrupt the reading because they feel that what they have to say is more important.

After that day, I became well known as a sensitive. Doing readings that way can be very draining. After several years of doing readings like that, I knew I needed to find another way to do readings that wasn't quite as tiring, so I asked my guides to help me find another way. In 2006, I was in the bookstore looking for another book about psychics, because even though I have never considered myself to be one, I was going through a lot of the same things that they did. Reading books by psychics helped me to realize what I was doing wrong in certain situations.

On this particular day while I was looking at a book on the top shelf, a box of cards fell down and I knew that they now belonged to me. They were called "Vibe Cards", and I have been using them for my readings ever since. Then at the beginning of 2010, I started using the vibe cards and a picture of a client (when they couldn't be there) and doing the reading from the essence of the picture. So far, it has worked out well. If you seek guidance and ask for the angels or spirit guides help, you will get it. Don't always expect it to happen overnight, but the answer will come to you. I always tell people to look for the signs.

My mom, Eulalia Allen (far right) with my brother Tomorris,
my niece Shirol and my sister Linda, at the clubhouse.

CHAPTER 9

Okay, Mom, It's Time to Cross Over

Dear old Mom, I miss her so. We used to talk on the phone at least every other day. It's good to have someone to talk to who will actually listen to how crappy your day has been. In the fall of 2000, my sister Jackie and her daughter Tiffany had been living with Mom. This was great, because my siblings and I knew that someone was always there with her.

One day, Mom stepped wrong and hurt her foot, so she had to be taken to the emergency room. After the X-rays were done, the doctor told the nurse to put a cast on the leg, from the foot all the way up to just below the knee. Now, I am not a doctor, but looking at all the thick varicose veins that mom had on her legs, I would have had a second thought about covering them up with a heavy cast. This cast was so tight and heavy that besides it hurting her, she had to use a walker to get around. She was miserable, and it pissed us off.

She had an appointment to see an orthopedist the week after the cast was put on. I was the manager over the Moderate and Intimate Apparel Department at the time, so during my lunch break, I took Mom to her appointment. This wonderful doctor took that cast off and did another X-ray on her foot and found no fracture. He put her foot in an ankle support brace. The orthopedist asked us why in the world the hospital had put a leg cast on a foot injury (over-billing and malpractice, we figured). When we left the office, I could tell that Mom felt much better, so I asked her if she was hungry. We went to the drive-thru at Burger King, and then I dropped her at home and headed back to work. When I called her that night, she said her leg and foot felt much better.

Saturday night, September 30, I called to check on Mom again. She said she felt okay but her leg felt a little hot. I asked if she wanted to go back to the emergency room (a different one, of course), and she said if it got worse, she would call me back. My mind went to the worst scenario, a blood clot, but I knew I had to have faith. Jackie and Tiffany were at the Dixie Classic fair and they would be home soon. The next morning, Sunday, October 1, Jackie called to say that mom had died early that morning. Jackie had spoken with Mom when she and Tiffany had got back from the fair. Mom had been eating a banana sandwich and watching TV.

By the time I got to Mom's house on Sunday, the paramedics were waiting for her doctor to come to the house. I had to go find my sister Michelle, she was at church, to tell her what had happened and get her back to the house. The paramedics took mom's body to the morgue, and we asked for an autopsy to be done. We buried her on October 5, four days after she had died at the age of 73.

Two weeks later, my husband and I and our two children left on our trip to Thailand. Chart's sister was getting married. Believe me, this was the worst trip ever. My mom had just died, and I was in Thailand trying to act like I was happy and excited about my sister-in-law's wedding. Then to top it all off, Chart was still spending money to pay for his sister's gown and rooms for her guests.

Chart had been sending money to his sister for about a year, and to arrive there and still be paying for stuff bothered me. I was pissed, and I cried every night. Chart's sister even had her own personal makeup artist who followed her around to keep her makeup touched up. How many brides do you know who have had that? Of course, if you are not the one who is shelling out the money, it's easy to come up with all these ridiculous things. On that trip, I was disappointed in my husband for letting himself be manipulated by his sister, especially after I had warned him about how she was. I spent as much time on that trip as I could in temple. That was my only solace, my peace of mind; it kept me from saying some pretty choice and unkind words to my husband and his sister. Besides my time in temple, the flight home was the happiest part of the trip for me. When we touched ground at PTI airport in Greensboro, I felt a tear roll down my face. This was going to be a rough holiday season.

Several weeks later, around 3:00a.m., one day, the doorbell rang. It startled me. Chart had left to throw his papers, so I tiptoed to the door and looked through the peephole, but no one was there. I went to the side door and found no one there either. I was tired, so I must have been hearing things, I figured. A few nights later, it happened again. It had officially become unnerving. I hate it when the phone rings that early in the morning, also, because I assume something bad has happened.

Well, a couple of weeks before Christmas, the doorbell rang again and I got up to see who it was. This time when I looked through the peephole, I realized it was Momma, so I opened the door and told her to come in. Once I did that, she just disappeared. I felt bad, though, of all people, this was my mother; I should have recognized her immediately.

Eventually, I went back to bed and fell back off to sleep and had a dream about being in the back yard of Mom and Dad's house on 17th Street. Growing up, my sister Millie and I had slept in the back room of that house. I had loved this room because Dad had put glow-in-the-dark stickers of the stars and the solar system on the ceiling. I slept on the top bunk (Millie made me), and that was cool because it put me up close to Venus and Mars.

Sorry, back to the dream. I was in the back-yard, and I opened the door that lead into our room, and Momma was standing in the corner, with her back to me. She was wearing a three quarter-length white gown, and I asked her if she was okay. She didn't respond. I walked closer, then suddenly, the room got darker and I was such a chicken that I started shaking. I love scary movies, and whenever something like this happens in a movie, I always say, "People are so stupid. Why don't they run?" Well, I didn't run.

Mom put up her hand and said, *"Stop."*

"Momma, please let me help you, are you hurt," I said.

As I tried to get closer, she came across that room so fast, that I almost peed my pants. *"You can't help me,"* she said, and then she flew back to the corner and I woke up. I cried because she had let me know that there was nothing any of us could have done. I'm sure Jackie had wondered, like me, if there was anything we could have done.

When my siblings and I and all our families got together at Mom and Dad's house that Thanksgiving like we always did for the holidays, I told the family about the doorbell ringing at the exact same time each night, about me getting up at 3:00a.m., and finally seeing Mom and about the dream. My sister's were having the same problem with their doorbells ringing and no one being there, especially at Mom's house. Yvonne said she had told Jackie who it probably was and to just let her in. As we were all standing there talking about this, the doorbell rang. We all stood still, and my brother Tomorris said, "Ya'll need to stop with all that ghost stuff." He went to answer the door and found some man who was hungry, asking for food. My brother Chris, started fixing the man some food, and we got him a drink and some dessert. He thanked us for the food and sat on the porch and ate.

Dear ole Dad had started the tradition of never turning away a hungry person who came to our door during the holidays. Our father had been in the Army and liked to cook big, like he was trying to feed a platoon of hungry soldiers. There was always more than enough to go around, and we all always took plates home for the next day. I especially liked taking home dressing. Dad made the best dressing I have ever tasted. He would mix it up in a big tub pot, then use his hands to smash it up, then put it in a long pan, smooth it out with his hands, and bake it. In 35 years, no one has been able to top it. Dad died in 1977. After the hungry man had left, Linda said, "Knowing Daddy, he could have been that old man at the door, just keeping an eye on us, to see if we are still abiding by his wishes."

My sister Michelle's face looked like she was thinking, *Whoa, I am in a family with a bunch of spooky sisters.*

After the first of the year (2001), some of us ended up at Jackie's(Mom and Dad's house) and finished talking about our ghost stories, as Tomorris put it. We were sitting in the living room with the door open because it was sunny outside. All of a sudden, the doorbell rang. The door was wide open, and we could see no one was there, so I got up and said, "We need to let her in. She doesn't realize that she is dead." I opened the door and said, "Come in, Momma."

After that encounter, I read a book about helping a loved one to crossover. When I got up the nerve, I explained to Mom that she had died in the room beyond the kitchen, where she slept most of the time, and had been found on the floor. She had looked very peaceful, like maybe she had laid there to take a rest, but never woke up. "Momma you need to crossover; it's time to crossover," I told her. She didn't say anything. I can't imagine how confused she must have been. I sensed that she was worried that the family would fall apart, people would go their separate ways, but I promised that I would do all that I could to keep the family strong in her absence. Daddy and all her other family members were waiting for her, I told her," So go, Momma, it's okay." She turned and slowly disappeared. You know, I have never seen anyone walk into the light. They just fade away. Now, I have seen a door and people come through the door, but I haven't seen anyone go back through a door. Hopefully, one day, our Heavenly Father or the angels will let me be able to view that most brilliant light, while helping another lost soul to cross over.I prayed that it had worked. The doorbell ringing stopped.

Good-bye, Momma. Tell everybody we miss and love them.

The family and Pilar's friend Shaunita, at Chilwadee's wedding in Thailand
(in October after mom's death)

Younger brother Wasun, shown, far left

Chapter 10

Grandma Allen's Grave

I guess it was maybe a little over a year after Momma passed, when I started getting the urge to find my grandma Allen's grave. It always happened around April or Easter-time. I would drive up toward Clemmons and go the way I remembered us driving to go to church with my dad each Sunday before he died (12/6/1977). My dad had buried his mom (Delpha Allen) at this small black church there called Capernaum Church of Christ, but I was never able to find it. The urge would go away after Easter, then come right back the next year, at the same time. My husband started driving up there with me because he realized I was becoming obsessed with it. This went on year after year. We were asking all the older people we knew if they had heard of the church, and they said, "Oh yes. Just keep straight, get off so- and-so exit, turn left, go down about two miles, "but we never found the church.

Then in 2006, after five years of searching for her grave every year around Easter, I had decided that this would be my last year. I know things like this made Chart think I was a little wacky, but I couldn't help it. So once again on my day off, I headed onto I-40, got off at the Clemmons exit, and just drove and drove, until I came to a side street before the dead end. I made a left and kept going straight until I got to Styers Ferry Road. I pulled into a little eating place on the right to compose myself because I was so frustrated and still no church in sight. Then a little old white man drove up in his car and got out to go get something to eat, and I thought, *Oh what the hell, he looks like a nice person.* So I got out of my car and approached him.

"Sir," I said, "I am so lost. My grandmother's grave is at a little church in Clemmons called Capernaum Church of Christ. I believe it's one of the oldest black church's here. Have you heard of it?"

He said, "Baby, sure I have. It's right down Styers Ferry to the right. You're just a few minutes away." Thank you, God, for this angel! After thanking the man profusely (I wanted to kiss him on his little bald head), I headed out on my journey in anticipation of finally reaching my destination. My hands were shaking, my heart was full of emotion. Finally, I would be able to be near the woman who had bestowed this special gift upon me.

There it was, the little white church (trumpets, please). I made a right turn into the parking lot. A beautiful big sign said, "Capernaum Church of Christ."

All the graves were at the back of the church, and the caretakers had done a wonderful job of preserving all the headstones. The grounds were immaculately kept. I knew that the people at this church cared about those who had passed on. I am thankful to them.

I put a spray of red, white, and blue flowers on top of Grandma Allen's headstone (her birthday is July 4th), and I stood there and talked to her and apologized for neglecting my duties as her grandchild. I also apologized to my dad.

That day, I made a promise that I would continue to put flowers on Grandma Allen's grave on Mother's Day, her birthday, Easter, and Christmas, and sometimes just because. I had been doing this for all my other family members who had passed on and who were buried at Evergreen Cemetery.

To this day, I don't know who was pulling on me so hard to find the grave Daddy or Grandma Allen. I did find out that the church had been in the paper the week that I finally found her grave (many thanks to the little man in the parking lot). The church people were worried about losing the church and about the graves being moved. Evidently, a guardian angel came through for them. Thank you, whoever you are.

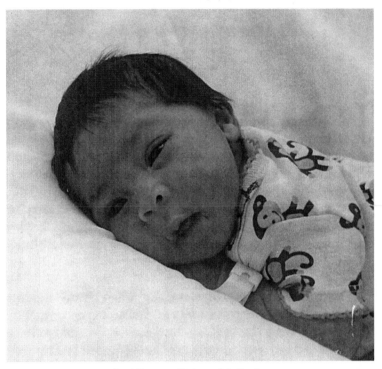

Jaiel Rattana Ridmee McCauley

CHAPTER 11

The Reincarnation of Rattana

In 2004, my son Priest, daughter-in-law Anika, grandson Daisean and granddaughter Gabrielle came down for the weekend from Virginia to visit. It was in April, but I can't remember if it was the Easter weekend or not. Early that Sunday morning, about 6:30, I awoke because I heard a child run down the hallway giggling. I got up out of bed and went to see if Gabby had gotten up and was playing. I didn't see her, so I opened their bedroom door to check on her and saw they were all still sound asleep.

I lay back down and started to doze off when I heard and saw this time, a little girl run down the hallway again, giggling. This time, I knew it wasn't Gabby, because she was two and this little girl looked to be around four years old, with shoulder-length straight jet-black hair and this little girl was definitely Asian and darker skinned. She actually looked like Pilar. Once everybody got up, we all talked about it but couldn't figure out who the girl was.

The next year, in April, it happened again. The little girl ran down the hallway twice, then just disappeared. Since I was the only one seeing her, I kept trying to figure out why I was seeing her. Was my daughter Pilar pregnant? Was I subconsciously

48

wanting to have a baby (was I crazy or on drugs)? Well, whatever the reason was, this mysterious phenomenon continued to happen each year in April for five years, through 2009. Then I realized who she was, my husband's baby sister. Chart had never spoken of her to me, because she had died in 1962, when she was only four months old (he was eight at the time) and his family had never known what caused her death, so he and his dad had put her small, delicate body in a wooden box and buried her at the temple in Kanchanaburi, by the Pagoda. Her death had been especially devastating, because she had been the first girl born to his parents.

Chart said in April of 1962, right after she died, a little flower appeared in her hand. His mom said she was an angel baby. My husband was eight when she died, he was adopted and came to the United States in 1970 and this was 2009, and he could not remember what his sister's given name was, so he called his younger brother Wasun and had him to ask their dad. His sister's name was Rattana. She had been born in December 1961 and died in April 1962 , that was why she kept coming around in the month of her death.

After, I acknowledged Rattana, she really started in on me. At night while I was sleeping, she would pull my covers down. When it first started happening, I thought that maybe I was getting hot during the night and pushing them down myself. Sometimes I do sleep hard, and I assumed this was what was happening.

During this same time, a little kitten started showing up on our door. We eventually took him in and named him Mokey. He was so cute, but all small animals are, it's when they get bigger that they become a pain in the butt. We let Mokey stay in the house, so most nights, he would jump into bed with us and snuggle in between my butt and knees. Well, after a while, this got on my nerves, so I made him get off the bed.

He stayed off for a few days, then jumped back up, but now he lay between Chart and me.

My covers kept being pulled down, somehow, and on one particular night, I awoke and saw Mokey lying over my feet. He did this several nights in a row, and when this got on my nerves, I put him off the bed again. We finally had to start closing the bedroom door to keep him from lying on top of my feet. I need my space. I didn't like Chart trying to hug on me all night, either, because I feel like I can't breathe. One night, Chart got up to check on the dogs, and when he returned to bed, he forgot to close the door, so slick little Mokey got back up on the bed and lay on my feet. You're probably wondering what the heck is wrong with that cat. In another life, maybe he was a human with a foot fetish, who knows? I woke up a little later to find him there, and I just gave up and let him stay there and I went back to sleep.

About an hour later, I awoke because he was making the awful sounds that cats make when they sense danger. I said, "Mokey, what is wrong with you?" Then he pounced on my feet and clawed the shit out of me. I screamed and kicked him off, then Chart woke up. I got up and went into the bathroom to see how bad it was. Mokey had clawed me pretty badly; there were blood, scratches, and little holes on the tops of both of my feet. The cat was still at the edge of the bed, making those noises, so I got a towel and hit at him until he ran out of the room. I told my husband, "No more Little Miss Nice Robbin." Mokey had drawn first blood, and it was on.

The next morning, I hopped around, acting like I was in much pain. I explained to Chart that after what that cat of his had done, I might not be able to walk right for a year and that mean cat needed to be put outside. Well, my sob story didn't work. Chart did start locking Mokey out of our room and did put him outside, but each evening, he would let the cat back in. At night, Mokey would scratch at the door, then he would get mad and start scratching at the carpet by our bedroom door. He was a lunatic, and when I saw how badly he had pulled up my carpet, I tried to beat the hell out of him with the broom, but he was too fast and I couldn't catch him.

Finally, one fateful night, I went to bed around 11:30. A little after midnight my covers were jerked completely off me. I jumped up in the bed and that was when I realized the person pulling down my covers was Chart's baby sister. I said, "Alright, Rattana, I am sick of this, stop it now." I got the covers and pulled them over me, so I could go back to sleep. Chart asked if I was okay. He was worried, and I was frustrated because Rattana wouldn't leave me alone. I lay back down onto my left side and eventually dozed off.

I thought I was dreaming, because I saw Rattana walk around to my back and put her hands on my back and then just step into my body. I jumped up out of the bed and said, "Oh God, no!" and ran to the bathroom. I flipped on the light and looked in the mirror. She was looking out through my eyes. I screamed and cried, "Chart, she's inside me. Oh no, oh no, please help me!" He didn't know what to do, and I was terrified. He sat up with me for awhile, trying to calm me down. Why had this happened? How had this happened? Was I dreaming? *Please wake me up, Lord, if I am dreaming*, I thought.

Chart had to go to work, and he asked me if I would be okay or if I wanted him to stay with me. I told him I was okay, but I wasn't. I wondered if I would ever be okay again. When he left, I turned on the TV and left the bedroom door open, hoping my enemy, Mokey, would come into the room with me because it was better than being alone. I called out for Mokey, and he came from out of the back bedroom, but when I tried to go towards him, he backed up and started with the hissing noises again.

So I went back to bed, and as I lay there, I realized that the cat was trying to let me know that there was a spirit at my feet. That's why he had attacked them, he was actually trying to protect me. Later that morning, every time I tried to get close to him, he would run away. He no longer saw me; he saw Rattana's spirit. It would remain that way until I got rid of her.

The next couple of weeks were very strained between me and my husband, because at first I couldn't see him as my lover. It felt more like I was living with my brother. When we hugged, it was nice and comforting, but when he kissed me on the lips, it was yucky.

Luckily, those feelings soon passed, and I started having dreams about Rattana. She was trying to let me know what had happened to her. In my dream, there were two long wooden boxes and she asked me to lie down in them with her, so I did. The boxes were made like coffins, and they ended up being too short, so our legs hung over the edges. This little girl was trying to let me know that her bones were in two different boxes, her bones had been separated. When I told my husband, he called his brother Wasun and asked him to check things out. Wasun called back later and told us that the pagoda that Rattana's little body had been buried beside had been moved and it was possible that Rattana's bones and a lot of other little babies' bones had gotten separated. This was heartbreaking for my husband to find out. Why would people move the bones and not be more careful, knowing that a lot of poor   families had buried their babies at that temple by that pagoda because they couldn't afford to bury them anywhere else?

By November 2009, Rattana' spirit had been inside me way too long. Since she had been with me, I had gained 20 pounds and was way past wanting to get rid of her, but I didn't know how, so I spoke with someone who told me that I needed to transfer her spirit into something else. I thought of a doll. I traveled from store to store and searched through lots of doll catalogs, thanks to another friend at work, but I couldn't find the Asian doll I was looking for. By December, because we couldn't find her in Winston, Chart and I decided to drive to Burlington Outlets. I headed straight back to the doll department. They had all types and nationalities of dolls, except Asian ones. Once again, I was disappointed, so I had to settle for one that looked only a little similar to that little four-year-old girl who kept running down my hallway. Maybe a Native American one would work. After walking all the way down past the last counter, I made the decision to leave. As I turned around, I noticed a doll with long dark hair, turned backward. I asked the clerk to let me see her. When Chart and I saw the doll, our jaws dropped. There she was, hidden and waiting for us. Wow! The clerk even commented that she had thought they had sold the last Asian doll the week before. But there she was, "Rattana", so we wrapped and boxed her up and took her home. The doll wasn't quite as dark as the little girl, but the features were eerily similar. Once we got the doll home, I asked for Rattana's spirit to please use this doll as her new vessel. I prayed and chanted, and she was released into the doll. "Thank you, Lord God, our Heavenly Father, for this blessing." I said.

At Christmas I showed her off to the family, I'm sure most of them thought I was a bit nutty, but who cares? Rattana was no longer in me, and that's all that mattered. After Christmas, I took her to work with me to let my ladies in better sports-wear, see her. Some of them knew what I had gone through and why I had purchased this special doll. They were curious to see how she looked and wanted to know if my husband thought she looked like his baby sister. When I brought her into the store, everyone who saw her was surprised by how lifelike she was. One of the girls commented that it looked like her eyes followed people.

I purchased her several different outfits (preemie) because I wanted to grow Rattana from an infant to four years old. I had to chop off some of the doll's hair and her bangs so her hair would fit inside of the preemie cap. She looked so pretty and lifelike that she was easy to love. I would give her hugs and kisses and even rock her when I got home from work. She remained on the couch in my relaxation room for months, except when Junie (my grandson) came over to spend the weekend with us. He had been born July 9 in 2007, so he was more than two years old when I got the doll, and for some reason, he did not like her near him. He said he didn't like her face and eyes, so I would box her up whenever he came over and bring her back out whenever he left.

In September of 2010, my daughter, Pilar, told me she was pregnant, and on May 19, 2011, Jaiel Rattana was born. Chart had asked Pilar if she would name the baby girl after his sister (because I had told him that I felt that Rattana was reborn into our new grandchild), but Pilar wanted both her kids' first names to begin with the same letter, J, so she made Rattana the girl's second name. This was funny, because I had done the same thing with my two children, but I gave mine the same three initials, PJC. I had this crazy notion that if I ever opened a business, I would name it PJC.

The day after Jaiel was born, the doll was put back into her box. I no longer needed to keep treating her like a child, because her soul was no longer there. Rattana had reincarnated in Jaiel. Months later, Gabby was at our house and she asked if she could play with the doll. Then I asked Gabby if she wanted take the doll home with her for a while. She said she did, but after a week or so, she called and asked me to pick the doll up because it was too much trouble, kind of like a real baby.

If Rattana had already been reborn into Jaiel, who was in my doll now? Gabby is going to be sensitive, too, and I know she sensed something, but I don't know what.

Surachart's parents in Thailand, Sumrit and Boonchoo Ridmee

CHAPTER 12

Don't Leave: Request from the Grave

In 2004, my husband's mother passed away in Thailand. Her name was Sumrit Ridmee. She was a small-framed woman, barely five feet tall, with a sixth or seventh-grade education, but she was a smart, strong woman who gave birth to twelve children, just like my mom. Our families had so many similarities, it was uncanny. Sumrit Ridmee even looked like my mother, just a much smaller version.

In 2005, my husband and I went back to Thailand to visit the family. I have always loved Thailand, the people, the waterfalls, the outside dances, and, of course, the real Thai food. This trip was going to be very strained, though, because immediately after Chart's mom had passed, his dad, Boonchoo, had got a girlfriend. Of course, Chart was livid when he found out. He took it as a disrespect to his mother and the family. The counselor part of me tried to explain to him that people react to death and being alone in different ways and maybe his father was with this woman because all of his kids had their own lives to live, we lived in the United States, and he just wanted a companion. Chart wasn't buying it, but he let it go.

I want to say something about my husband here. He believes in his family and only wants the best for them. That's why in 1998, we began sending money to Thailand to expand and update his parents' home. A store was added on in the front so they could sell food and groceries to live off of and not have to get up early each morning to cook food and be at the market to sell it by 3a.m. each day. They were in their 70's, and we felt it was time for them to start taking it easy. It wasn't until October 2000, that we had got to see what a wonderful job Chart's sister, Chilawadee, had been able to accomplish with the monies we'd sent home. Chilawadee, had got married that same year, so having the house look so good made his parents very proud. You will remember that one was a rough trip for me because I had experienced a lot of sadness and loss since July of that year: My son Priest's, first wife Tomica had died in a car accident on July 13 and we had found my mom dead at her house on October 1; we had buried Mom on October 5 and gone to Thailand a few weeks later.

Back to 2005 and Boonchoo and his girlfriend. She tried to stay away from the house during our visit. Once we got settled, we went sightseeing, but Chart's dad chose to stay home. I love shopping over there, because you can get great deals on jewelry, handbags, watches, and movies. Let me tell you I was in heaven!

Chart and I stayed in the newly remodeled back room. The bed went from one wall and almost all the way over to the other wall. We had air-conditioning and a TV with a VCR; that's all I needed. One night, after being there for about a week, I was tired and just wanted to relax and watch movies, so Chart went out with his sisters and brothers. While watching movies, I went through all the stuff I had bought so far. A little before midnight, I got tired, so I turned off the TV and fell off to sleep. Sometime later, Chart's mom came to me in a dream (I guess it was a dream). She told me not to leave. No matter what happened, I was not to leave that house. I said okay, then I lay back down on the bed and she lay behind me and put her arms around me. The funny thing was that Sumrit did not speak English, but I understood every word she said.

The next evening, we made plans to eat at an exclusive restaurant with all the family (our treat). I was in our room, getting ready, when I heard hollering going on outside our bedroom door. I opened the door. Chart was steaming mad and told me to pack my bags because we were going to a hotel. He said he had had it with his dad. When I said no, he said, "Robbin, pack your bags, because if I stay in this house another night with this man, I'm going to hurt him."

Chart's sisters were crying, and Wasun was trying to talk to his dad, so I pulled Chart into the room and told him about my visit/dream from his mom and why I couldn't leave. After calming down, he understood. His brother calmed his dad down, and they finally made up. We ended up having a great time.

The only other time I talked to Chart's mom was in 2012, during Chinese New Year. She asked for a certain flower to be put at her gravesite. I thought it was a flower she wanted Chart to get, but when I described it, he said that wasn't a flower here, but rather in Thailand, so he called Wasun and told him to get it for her.

CHAPTER 13

Almost Past-Life Regression

For many years, I had been thinking about having a past-life regression done. Like everybody, I had a lot going on in my life and I wondered if having this done might give me some answers to a lot of questions I had, such as why some people are doctors, teachers, murderers or why some are constantly sick, and, of course, why so few people are psychic or like me, so sensitive.

I didn't know of anyone who had actually had a past-life regression done, so I had to do some research to find the right hypnotherapist. My birthday was coming up, so I thought this would be a great gift to myself. There was a show on TV where people had this done, so I was hoping to find out if I remembered a life as a slave. But mine didn't quite work out that way.

After my almost past-life regression (as the hypnotherapist called it), she was able to help me to set some boundaries at work and make my life a little easier, at least for a while. Because of the length of the session and because it was very draining, it was also extremely emotional. The recording*of the regression is still very hard for me to listen to, and I thank my guide "Stephanie" for getting me through it.

*to listen to the tape, go to the website provided at the back of the book. *

Priest, 13 years old, and Pilar, 4 years old, standing outside
of our townhouse at Northill Townhouses

Chapter 14

Sensitive Children

Have you ever wondered if your child was highly sensitive or psychic? Well, I have. Nowadays, you hear a lot about psychics and sensitives, but when I was coming up, you didn't. No wonder most of us who were born sensitive's 40 to 50 years ago are so messed up. Growing up in a society where people thought you were weird, slow, timid, or Satan's spawn because you talked about dead people or had visions was hard.

Most psychics and sensitives, tend to stay to themselves. Not me. I had a big mouth, and I ran it all the time. (I still do, and it gets me into hot water quite a bit.) I talked so much that Miss Kat, my grandma McCoy's friend, use to call me bird. She said I was always chattering away in grown folks' conversations. She was right. The problem was that I understood grown folks better than I understood children my own age.

When I finally had my own two children, the question always lingered in the back of my mind whether they might turn out like me. My son, Priest, was a wonderful baby once he got past three months. He started sleeping through the night, he would stay with anyone, he played well with other children, and he talked all the time and would tell all our personal business. I looked for signs of him being psychic or sensitive, believe me, but he never showed any. Priest was a normal rough-and-tumble boy who broke his arm and then tried to go swimming with a cast on, got it wet, and tried to hide it.

Priest once tried to ride a ten-speed bike down a steep hill with no brakes, even after my brother Tomorris told Priest to let him ride it because his legs were longer and Priest could ride his bike, but Priest seemed to have his own agenda, in which he knew that he could stop his bike. Well, after being thrown to the pavement and having the top layer of skin on both arms ripped off, a huge hematoma on his forehead and a broken arm,(talked about earlier), all he could think about was what his dad was going to say. He asked my two brothers to help him to his bed upstairs, expecting that by the next day, everything would be right with the world. My brother Chris told Priest that Sayra (their nickname for my husband) was going to kill him.

Last, but not least, there was the white-car incident: Priest and my nephew Mandrill were out driving around and when they came back to the apartment complex, Priest tried to make a u-turn and hit the dumpster. After they got back to the house, my son applied whiteout to the damaged area to cover it up. He actually thought he had done a good job, but Pookie (Mandrill) told him that Sayra was going to kill him. Needless to say, Chart immediately noticed the whiteout. And when he called to tell me what Priest had done, we were both laughing so hard that Priest survived yet another day.

Now, my daughter, Pilar, was the opposite of her brother. From the moment she came home, she slept all night, but she was a holy terror when it came to letting someone else hold or take care of her. She was afraid of everyone. When she started daycare, the teacher said she would cry for the first 30 minutes after she was dropped off. Pilar did not want to play with other children, but she would play by herself. She was the same way at home, having tea with her imaginary friends (she may have seen them, but I never did), playing dress-up with her paper dolls, and watching cartoons; we would never hear a peep out of her. I would go check on her or send Priest in because she was too quiet.

Around four or five years of age, Pilar began to communicate with other human beings. Sorry, Pilar, just kidding. I did notice that she would never do things in front of an audience unless someone else was with her. Whenever her cousin Tandice would dance for us, Pilar would join in; she was a great dancer and still is. Priest was also a great dancer, and he loved Michael Jackson (we even bought him a red jacket and one silver glove). Priest could always get Pilar to dance. I remember when we lived at Northill Townhouses, off Indiana Avenue. This one Sunday before going to church with my aunt Thelma, they were in Pilar's room and Priest had on a pink shirt and grey pants and Pilar had on a white dress with a pink ribbon at the waist. He was playing a little guitar, and she was singing "Mary Had a Little Lamb" (a Kodak moment).

I did try to put Pilar in tap and ballet classes, but she ended up not liking them. Next, I put Priest and Pilar in a karate class together. Priest dropped out first, then Pilar followed. What a shame, too, Pilar was very limber and her teacher had said she was good. She could have been able to kick some butt like those Kung Fu fighters we use to go to the Ritz theater to see. Rest in peace, Bruce and Brandon Lee.

Some of the books out now would say that either one of my children could be sensitives, but I just never saw the signs. My granddaughter Gabby, however, definitely could be. In 2008, when her family moved into the house they are in now, she started having dreams about an old woman wanting to take her to the other side. Gabby was six years old at the time. Evidently, these dreams really bothered her, and so did this old woman. When my son finally told me, I went to the bookstore to get a book on what goes on, on the "other side." After reading the book, I told Gabby to tell this woman that she did not want to go play on the other side and to stop bothering her and to say loud and clear, "No, I don't want to go," several times and tell the old woman to "stop" coming to her, in her dreams. The dreams stopped, but Gabby is still showing lots of signs of being a sensitive child. Gabby told me that she senses people following her sometimes. She gets overwhelmed sometimes at the mall and prefers small gatherings to larger ones. Yes, I definitely feel that I need to keep a watchful eye out for my Gabster.

I think my grandson Jermelle Jr. (aka Junie), may be a sensitive child, because of something that happened not long after Chart's adoptive father, Wade Campbell died in September of 2009. Chart and I had Wade cremated and brought his ashes back to Winston-Salem with us.

Wade had lived in Washington, DC. Before he retired, he had been an architectural engineer for Metro Railway. He met my husband in Thailand in the 1960s, when he was stationed there building an airport and railway system. My husband had lived near Latya Village, in Kanchanaburi, Thailand. Wade was a major in the Army, which was a huge feat for an African American in the late 1960's. When Wade and Chart met, they became friends very fast.

Major Campbell's life was the service, so he never married, but he always put family first. Before he adopted Chart, his number-one concern had been taking care of his mother. He built her a home in Sharon, Pennsylvania.

A few months after Wade's death, Junie spent the weekend with us. Chart went to bed around 9p.m., but Junie wanted to stay up to watch a movie with me. Around 10:30p.m., he said he was tired and asked if I would warm up some milk for him. After he had his milk, I put him to bed. A little after midnight, I decided to call it a night. When I lay down in the bed, Junie said, "Hey, Gamma." I asked Junie why he was still awake. "I look at that man right there," he said. I asked what man. "That black man." I told him that I did not see any man and he should turn over and go to sleep. I hate it when anyone can see something that I can't see, because it makes me feel out of the loop.

Let me tell you about Junie. He turned five on July 9, 2012, but when this happened, he was two and a half and he thought he was white. His mom, Pilar, is white, his granddad and I are both white, and his uncle Preece (Priest) is too. His dad and great grandma Hazel were black, like the man in the corner that he saw. Where he got the black and white people information from, I don't know, but for him, anyone who was light-skinned was white and all dark-skinned people were black. The minds of children are amazing. After this happened several more times, I sensed that the man he was seeing was Wade, who was talking with Junie. I once showed Junie a picture of Wade, and he said, "Gamma, that's the black man in the corner." Then Junie just stopped seeing Wade.

Gabrielle, Jaiel Rattana and Jermelle Jr., at Priest's house

CHAPTER 15

Kristin and the Angel

Once a Belk associate named Kristin found out that I did readings and sometimes saw things, she couldn't wait to sit down and talk to me. She was very spiritual, so we ended up having a lot in common. Whenever I went past her at work, she would ask, "Do you see anyone around me?" and I would always say no. Then she would ask, "But you would tell me, right?" I told her that yes, I would definitely tell her if I saw someone around her.

My gift doesn't work quite like that, on demand. I am not a psychic or medium. I am a sensitive, so I can sense things about people. Some people have a wall up saying "Stop, don't read me," so I don't. With any gift, you have to learn to respect people's feelings. Honestly, this is fine with me. What bothers me is when people think that I go around all day knowing exactly what's happening to everyone. If I could do that, I would not be wasting my time in retail. I would be using that talent and making some big bucks. Think about it, if I could pick up stuff off everyone I came in contact with on a daily basis, I would have to be admitted to a mental asylum.

The moment I walked through the door at Belk, my senses went into overdrive. I started picking up illnesses, marital problems, work frustrations. And some associates had spirits attached to them. For me this meant that I could sense if it was male or female, young or old, so I knew this is exactly where I was destined to be at that phase of my life. I was guided to Belk for a reason, so I made the most of it. After telling Kristin that I had to calm myself from within to be able to work there, she said she wanted to try that also; she felt so stressed and thought that was what was contributing to her back pain.

In January of 2011, Kristin had back surgery and was having a lot of pain after, making it hard for her to get around. After performing inventory, I took my first vacation from January 15 to 23. I was scheduled to return on Monday the 24th (Priest's birthday). On my vacation, I worked on early spring cleaning and did some shopping, and that Saturday, Chart and I went to Greensboro to eat some Thai food and look for a rabbit statue for our home. My husband and I are practicing Buddhists and he is part Thai and Chinese, so we always look for an animal that represents the Chinese Zodiac. Starting February 3, 2011, it would be the year of the rabbit. We ate and then went across the street to a Korean market to see what they had. We walked around the market but couldn't find a single rabbit statue.

After we had looked further around the market, we went into an angel shop. Being an angel junkie, I was like a child in a candy store; I couldn't make up my mind what I wanted. The store had clocks, blankets, and pictures, but none of them jumped out at me, so we left. As we walked past the angel store, something made me turn around, and that's when I saw her. She was turned backwards and I couldn't see her face. I asked the owner if she was for sale, and he said, "How did she get back there?"

When I saw the angel's face, I said, "Oh my God, Chart, she is so enchanting and big!" She had shoulder-length blonde hair; a flowing dress of pink and lime green and wings of lavender, yellow, and pale green. I took her home and cleansed her and decided that she would be perfect in my office. This angel was special, but at the time, I didn't know just how special she would end up being.

The next day, Sunday the 23rd, I headed to work to check my e-mails and clear up some paperwork. I went in through the entrance closest to my office (which I rarely did). Jaclyn, another Belk associate, was sitting on the side wall, crying. She told me that Kristin had died. Kristin had told me what a great friend Jaclyn was and how Kristin loved the Estee Lauder cosmetic ladies. She felt very lucky to have these people in her life. You know, I have had to deal with a lot of death in my life, of people close to me and of the people who have passed over who come to see me. Being the way I am, I quickly learned to adapt, but whenever someone so young, like Kristin, who was 27 dies, it makes me question (like everybody else) if the short time they did have was fully lived. Kristin's was. Her life may not have been long, but she was able to touch many lives during it. A person's life is not measured by how long they have lived but by how many people they loved or shown compassion for while here on this earth. Kristin knew this, and I feel that's why she was so wild and carefree. She understood that she had to fill her short life with enough heartache and pain, love and understanding, compassion and kindness to encompass a lifetime.

Kristin was laid to rest on Friday, January 28, 2011, at 4:00 p.m. All of the ladies at the Belk counter attended her funeral. The next week, Kristin came to me, but I couldn't understand what she was trying to tell me. You see, for me, those who visit me don't actually speak. They communicate in something like telepathy, and I feel that because I am not a psychic, I tend to be slower at getting the messages spirits are trying to relay to me. Finally, after several days, I understood what Kristin needed me to do for her before she could complete her mission. There was a picture of her and the Estee Lauder ladies inside a book that she kept in the spa room. She wanted me to put it on the kiosk counter so she would be with them when they hit the $2 million dollars in sales, for the store. When these phenomenal ladies did it, Kristin was right there with them, like she had said she would be. Everybody was wondering how the picture had gotten put at the counter. After I explained to them about Kristin's visit, we realized that Kristin's message was an amazing spiritual experience for all of us.

One month later, after the counter hit the $2 million in sales, it was Estee Lauder's gift time. Sophia, the Estee Lauder counter manager and another one of Kristin's friends, was getting ready for work and, of all things, she had a desire to wear pink eye shadow and lipstick. Now, Sophia said that she didn't really like pink and never wore pink, but that day, she was compelled to do so. All of the ladies at the EL cosmetic counter wore pink tops that day to help promote the start of their new gift with purchase, which just happened to contain all of Kristin's favorite colors (shades of pink). Around noon, I came in and walked past the counter to the elevator. I pushed the up button, to call it to level two. While I was waiting, I turned towards the Estee Lauder counter and what I saw immediately made my heart start beating so fast that my hands began to shake. When the doors opened, I stepped in, but I continued to stare in disbelief at Kristin with the girls at the cosmetic counter. I sat in my office for awhile, trying to figure out how to explain to the ladies that Kristin had been standing at the register as the girls were ringing up their customers.

After getting up the nerve to go back downstairs. I walked over to Sophia and Amanda, another Estee lauder cosmetic associate and asked if I could speak to them for a moment. Kristin was in a "flowing dress in pale pink, light green, and yellow, and her shoulder-length blonde hair was blowing as if a small breeze had come through; she was glowing. As I told Sophia and Amanda that their beloved Kristin was standing in the kiosk, watching them, they hugged each other and reminded me that what I described her as wearing made sense because her obituary was printed in yellow and pink.

Kristin stayed there for a long time, just watching them, then she was gone. Later, when I returned to my office, I looked at her obit. Then I glanced over at the new angel that I had purchased the day before her death, and it blew my mind. That angel had blonde hair and was wearing a flowing dress in light pink, green, and yellow. From that day forth, to me, this angel has represented Kristin and her pure soul.

In honor of Kristin, funds were raised and the "Kristin Blair Charles" Playground was built. Like I said, a person's life is not enriched by how many years they lived but by how many lives they have touched during their time here on Earth.

In Memory of Kristin Blair Charles
September 2, 1983-January 23, 2011

CHAPTER 16

Walking the Labyrinth: Insight into My Spiritual Path

When we were in Thailand, I saw people walking a huge labyrinth. At that time, I really didn't think much about it, but as the years went by, my inner self became more spiritual and so I was always looking for ways to increase my insight into my next journey in life. In December of 2011, the Maitreya Project came to Winston-Salem, of all cities, and I was able to attend the viewing of all the ancient Buddhist relics, and on January 22, 2012, I would be walking an indoor labyrinth at the Kate Biting Hospice. You know how people talk about being in the right place at the right time? Well, that's what happened. In December of 2011, I had been visiting a friend's father at the hospital to do Reiki treatments on him; in January, he was sent to hospice. Once he was moved over there, I started visiting him there to do treatments.

I don't always do well in places where people have died, so I was sort of leery about going there. A year or so before, I had gone to the same hospice to visit another friend, who had worked at Belk, Juanita, and when I had walked into her room, I had seen two spirits up in the corner of her room, a male and female dressed in clothes from the early 1900's, so I didn't know if they were family or just messengers who had come to be with her prior to her passing. Juanita had seemed fine, and we had great conversations about people at work. She had even been eating some candy that another Belk associate, Gwen, and her two grandsons had brought. I had told Juanita that I would be back to see her again in a few days, but the very next day, she turned for the worse and one of my co-workers who went to see her said Juanita had been talking to people in her room but no one was there. Juanita died the day after that, so you can see how I might not be so crazy about visiting people at hospice. But I liked Mr. Gerald and planned on visiting him after my walk.

Because I had never walked a labyrinth before, I went on the Internet to see what I needed to do to prepare for it. The morning I was going to walk, before I took my shower, I sat down at my altar and prayed and asked for blessings while on my journey. I asked for all of my spirit guides' help. As I left the altar to take my shower, I walked past the pictures of members of our family who are now deceased, and I asked for their help also. While in the shower, I always wash my hair, then just stand under the water, close my eyes, and let the water roll down my face. Besides being relaxing for me, water washes away all negative energy or trash (as I call it) that I pick up from people daily, but this time, something happened that had never happened before. A door opened, and spirits started coming through. First came Wade (my husband's adoptive father); then Chart's biological mother, Sumrit; then my mom, Eulalia; my dad, John Henry; and finally, Warren (my son-in-law's grandfather). With my eyes closed, I kept trying to get my brother Harold and my maternal grandparents, Mary and John McCoy, to come through, but they never did. Of course I jumped out of the shower to tell my husband what had just happened. Ten years before, Chart probably would have taken me to the loony bin once I'd explained about all my visitors, but after I had told him about his mother's death minutes before he had learned of it from his brother Wasun, he had become open to the potential of my special gift and had even started telling his family and friends about me. After I told him about everyone who had come through, he admitted that he had been praying to them also, but for a different reason. Wow, that was pretty amazing, what the two of us could do! I will never forget that special experience.

I got dressed and headed out to the indoor labyrinth. While driving there, I kept thinking about my visitors, then out of nowhere, I started smelling mothballs. The smell got stronger and stronger, then I realized that my grandma Mary McCoy had come through to help me also. Thank you, Grandma. I was nervous when I walked through the door. The lady at the front desk asked me if I needed any help walking the labyrinth, but I told her that I already had enough people helping me out. I took several deep breaths to slow my breathing and transition myself from this life to my spiritual journey. All jewelry and shoes must be removed, and after I removed mine, I bowed my head and said a prayer to show respect some people recite affirmations. I walked very slowly inward with my hands clasped behind my back, putting one foot in front of the other, letting go of all things that I wanted to discard, breathing in the exhilaration of each and every step.

Once I reached the center, I sat in the chair and continued to pray and contemplate what I wanted to come away from this experience with. My mind suddenly became very peaceful and quiet.

Whoa, this is the only time my mind has actually been silent, I thought. *Buddha bless.*

Then I got up to take the return path, holding in my heart all the love and compassion that I wanted to bestow upon the world. As I slowly arrived at the end of my journey, I turned, bowed my head, and gave thanks. I felt lighter, and I had answers to where my mission would take me next.

My baby brother, Harold

CHAPTER 17

Harold's 40-Year Visitation

O n the morning of March 11, 2012, a Sunday, I got out of bed around 9:45a.m. Normally, I don't sleep this late, but my body was tired. After getting up, I went to get my vitamin drink, Carabao (a product from Thailand, it means buffalo) and a large glass of water and headed to my room to watch a movie. I wanted to watch *"Ghostrider".* I put it in the DVD player, but it wouldn't play. I pushed the disc in two more times, and it popped back out. *Well, I guess my spirit guides don't want me to watch a movie, so I'll watch TV instead,* I thought. Of course, I turned it to channel 625, Chiller, my nephew Tory introduced me to it, and now I am hooked. Tory and I both love to watch Chiller because it has scary movies and supernatural stuff on all the time. That day was no exception. *"Children of the Grave"* a documentary, was coming on at 10:00a.m. Thank you, spirit guides. The documentary really hit home because I had been doing a lot of readings in the past year that involved children little ones whose souls hadn't passed over, forgotten children.

This episode focused on haunted hospitals where kids had died and on   cemeteries and other places where there had been tragedies involving children. I became so enthralled in the show that at 11:55a.m., when it was ending, I realized that I had forgotten to eat breakfast. As I started to get up, a coldness came over the right side of the room by my big "angel" that sits on the floor. I got up and walked towards the door; it was warmer there. Then I went back to the "angel" and felt there was still a chill in that area. Of course someone was there, but who? I called Chart to come to the room to see if he felt the same thing. He did, but he thought maybe a cool breeze was coming from the window or the vent, so we checked out both. No luck; it was definitely an upset spirit.

The room was getting so cold that I could see my breath. My right hand had started to hurt because of the temperature change in the room. I went out into the hallway to check the thermostat it said 70 degrees. Now, I had to find out who this person was, because I had never experienced coldness like this when I had had my other visitors. I got a comforter, put on my gloves, and wrapped my winter scarf around my head and ears and over my nose, determined to stay put until I figured out who was causing this.

After I had frozen for about 30 more minutes, my baby brother Harold started materializing. But he wasn't alone. Evidently, he was mad because I had not remembered his birthday the day before, March 10 and I had not put any flowers on his grave. He made me feel even worse because we had celebrated Yanni's birthday (my niece Shirol's daughter) at my niece Karen's boyfriend's house. We had a great time my sister Yvonne, Shirol's oldest daughter, Mahogany; Yvonne's son Mandrill and his wife Christina and their children; Karen's daughter Myesha and her kids; Karen's youngest daughter Tarshika, my spiritual buddy, and Yvonne's son Richard, Jr., and I had just forgot about Harold's birthday. I am the one who is always telling people not to forget about the dead. "Go put flowers on their grave, talk to them, let them know you care," I always say that. No doubt, I had fallen down on my job.

Harold was pulling me to go to Butner, where he had died, and to help release his soul and maybe the little boy named Marshall, who was with him. Marshall looked to be around six and was dark-skinned and had a short afro and brown eyes. Harold and Marshall had both died at the Murdoch Center, but I don't know if it was in the same year (Harold was 12 when he died). Since 2010, I had seen children pass on and grow and had been able to tell the parents or grandparents how they were adjusting to being on the other side. But Harold hadn't aged; he still looked 12. Of course, had he gotten older, I may not have been able to recognize him.

I knew I had to go to Butner, North Carolina for my brother. The room started to warm up, and Harold and Marshall slowly disappeared. I checked the thermostat in the hallway again. I don't even know why I did it, but I put my finger on the top and I felt their energies pass thru me and the temp rose to 90 degrees, then I took my finger off and it went back down to 70. I pulled Harold's obituary from my family album and went online to look up the Murdoch Center and to find out if it was still in Butner. It was, and in the exact same place 40 years later. Chart was so wonderful and understanding that he took me to Butner on Saturday March 17 so I could take flowers to the chapel for Harold and Marshall and bid their souls farewell. My granddaughter Gabby (Priest's daughter) went with us. It was a memorable day.

In Memory of Harold Martinez Allen
March 10, 1960 – April 15, 1972

CHAPTER 18

Reiki and the Healing Hands

A round 2006, I started learning and doing Reiki, which is a Japanese form of healing touch that means "universal life energy." Because I used to do my readings by holding a person's right hand, I felt Reiki was right up my alley. I learned about Reiki while browsing at the book-store; my hands seem to know exactly which books to pull out, and I rarely have to stay in a bookstore more than 20 minutes when I am looking for a book on the paranormal or psychic abilities. Over the years, I have read books by some great authors who have helped me understand my gift better, including Echo Bodine's (my favorite)" *The Gift*", "*Echoes of the Soul*", "*A Still Small Voice*," and "*Hands that Heal*"; Allison Dubois's (no, not the medium on TV, played by Patricia Arquette, but the real person the TV show is based on) "*Secrets of the Monarch*" and "*We Are Their Heaven*"; Sylvia Browne's (her books are hard for me to grasp, she is so far out there) "*Phenomenon*" and "*Life on the Other Side*" (which I read because I was trying to find out about the other side when Gabby was having dreams about it, as I mentioned earlier).

Once I got home with my book about Reiki, I started reading it and couldn't put it down. I knew this was something that would come naturally to me. When I started practicing Reiki on people, I knew I would need to touch them, so I incorporated light touch massage with Reiki. I would smooth out their auras and work to balance their chakras. Immediately, heat (energy) would come from my hands and I knew that I had found a spot that needed healing touch. From the very beginning, I did Reiki on people with my eyes closed. With my eyes closed, I can see in my mind the colors that emanate from a person's body. I have seen orange, red, green, and black. I make them cover their eyes so they won't think that a crazy woman is working on them. When people are receptive to the healing, it can usually help them, but if I feel that there is a serious problem, I tell them to go see a doctor. While I am scanning a person's body and I feel a hot place, I will hold my hand on the area to try to cool it. If it continues to be hot, I start a circling motion to try to bring the heat up and out. This is not I repeat, is not traditional Reiki movement, but this works for me, and the friends and family members I have worked on like it. They especially love the massage, even though it is very light helping my daughter Pilar study when she was going to school to be an esthetician gave me the opportunity to learn about pressure points.

I love practicing on people who are under a lot of stress or who have minor aches and pains and I love being able to make them feel more relaxed. For me, learning Reiki was another part of my mission as a healer. I do like helping people and listening to what some of them experience while we transfer the life energy back and forth. I become as energized as they do. My first real test of the healing effect that Reiki can have on the body came when my younger brother Chris was in a really bad car accident. During the times that I stayed with him, once he was released from the hospital, I would do Reiki on his back and legs. He said it always felt relaxing and made his legs feel better. Our family and Chris's girlfriend Lisa's main concern was to get him back up on his feet. Of course, I knew Chris would be okay because my spirit guides had already told me when my siblings and I arrived at the hospital, after the accident. My spirit guides said he had such a strong will and body. Our dad's spirit was at the hospital and by Chris's bed during the really tough days and nights. I don't know if Chris remembers, but Chris's soul was looking down at him in the hospital and kept saying, "Wake up, Chris, you have to wake up. Your body is strong and your will is strong and you can make it through this." My family is amazing, and so was Chris's girlfriend, Lisa (his wife now). With Lisa and Dad's help, my siblings and I all learned how to care for Chris and how to assist in his recovery process. My younger sister Michelle did a phenomenal job in taking care of all of Chris's financial matters, once he was home. And I don't want to forget to also thank my sister Millie for bringing in pictures of the family to stick on the wall so when Chris did wake up from his coma, he would know that his family was with him at all times.

Years later, I would work with Mr. Gerald, by request of his daughter, Princess. While I worked with him, he taught me a lot about transcendental meditation. I worked on Mr. G for months (this was a life test of learning to make sure that I must always ground myself and clear away all negative energies and any illness that I may have picked up from the receiver, after each session). If you continually get sick after doing the treatments, it is time for you stop at least that is how I felt. I had become too attached or he was stronger than I thought he was and had started pushing his illness back onto me (not deliberately). Mr. Gerald was a smart, intelligent man. I wish I had had the opportunity to meet him years before.

Some doctors are finally realizing how beneficial Reiki can be, and I hope the insurance companies will figure this out too. Reiki is a great stress reliever, and with what most companies require their employees to deal with daily, especially management, it's no wonder people end up having strokes, constant migraines, and back and shoulder pain. All these are due to stress on the job. I know my co-workers from my job are stressed, and I get frustrated from being overwhelmed by everything the managers are expected to be able to do.

Hopefully, my guides will let me know when it is time for me to move on to the next phase of my life path, going back to school so I can start my own business or work in a women's wellness center. I would love to work on patients who are extremely nervous prior to major surgery; being able to relax could be very beneficial to their recovery process.

Chapter 19

Powers of Protection

My powers of protection are things that I do to protect my home, car, office, family, and self. One of the best things I did for myself was to have an altar built by my friend Jackie, who is an extremely talented woodworker. My husband and I renewed our vows for our 30th anniversary. I wanted to do it all in the Thai tradition, and having the altar built was the finishing touch. Jackie also does photography, so she took the pictures for the ceremony. My altar is my holy place of worship and where I send out blessings and prayers of healing to family and friends. (Whenever I do readings and the prayer card comes up, I explain to people how important it is to pray, daily. We should all give thanks for making it through another day and for waking up each morning.)

Being a practicing Buddhist and not having a temple close by makes me thank Jackie each day for giving me my altar and realize how amazing it is that people come into our lives at the right time. My altar holds a 100-year-old Buddha statue from my mother-in-law, Sumrit Ridmee, and is adorned with flowers, scented soaps, dried fruit, ivory and gold decorations, and pictures of my family.

Flat mirrors are on all windowsills throughout the house. They need to be kept clean to keep negative energy out. I put sponges in each room, one at the entrance to my home, two in the dining area where I usually do all my readings, one on the headboard in our bedroom, one in the guest bedroom, one in my quiet room (the room I go to get away from the worries of the world), and one on the windowsill in the kitchen. I also keep a sponge in my office at Belk and in my car. If I don't keep the one at work properly cleansed, then the trash from work will stick to me and physically drain me. (Trash is built-up energy that people unload while talking to me. The sponge absorbs this left over energy, so I won't stay drained.) The sponges help to keep me grounded. I cleanse them in cool water and sea salt. Most of my crystals are cleansed this way also. To dry my crystals, I blow on them, which keeps my energy on them.

Of course, my angels also protect me, and my spirit guides help to guide me in the right direction. My angels will only let me go to the other side when my mission has been completed here on Earth. (I hope that I have many, many years before this happens.) I have a large angel statue in my office that reminds me of my friend Kristin, and I wear an angel pin and watch whenever I need that extra closeness or guidance from my angels.

In my quiet (relaxation) room in my home is a large statue of an angel that stands on the floor, dressed in pink and holding a white dove and candle. One entire shelf in my hutch displays all the angels I have acquired over the years. Another shelf displays statues of my African American heritage and the bottom shelf displays my Native American side. My sofa cover is a lavender-and-purple print, and my curtains are purple. I love being surrounded by purple because it is a color that I feel protects me from negative people and spirits. How do I know this? An angel told me.

Many years ago, I had a wonderfully enlightening dream of walking through   a beautiful field and seeing a light. Of course, I went towards the light and found it was an "angel", draped in a purple cloak with white and gold trim. The angel's face was pure white light, so I couldn't see any facial features, but from the voice, I knew that the angel was female. All she said was that purple would be my spiritual color (a color that protects me), that it would bring me much peace in my life and would help my gift. She was right.

I have had no more dreams about angels, but after that dream, I did see four   angels hovering above the ladies' shoe department at work, one afternoon. Them being there scared me. They were there for three or four days. I am not a Bible reader, but I love my God and I needed to find out why those angels were there at the shoe department, so I spoke to many people at work. Some said it could be a warning, others said the angels could be keeping a watch over me or the store. When the angels finally left, I worried about it for many weeks. Was it my time and were they my guides to the other side? Then I just had to let it go. Nothing bad happened, so I guess they were just keeping watch.

Getting back to my relaxation room… I have Native American and African American pictures and objects on the walls. Lastly, there is a four-shelf metal stand that holds a Buddha given to me by the ladies in Better Sportswear (I have great friends throughout the store), and several Asian dolls from another associate, who brought them to me when she went home to visit her family overseas. I also carry encased Buddha's in my handbag, for daily protection and to keep me close to my faith.

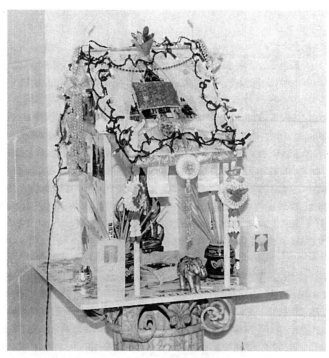

My alter at my home (built by Jackie Briggs)

CHAPTER 20

The Connection of Three

I really thought that "Powers of Protection" would be my final chapter, but I was wrong. After an incident on July 31, 2012 my spirit guides informed me that this chapter would be my ending. Chart had to have a procedure done, and I needed to go with him because he was going to be sedated. I usually wake up around 7:30 or 8:00 in the morning. My normal routine is to get my vitamin drink and a large glass of water and sit down to read the newspaper, but that morning, I was told to get my Bible and go through the obits in it. When my mom was alive, she would always put the obituaries of family, friends, and her favorite actors in her bible, and when she passed on, I kept her tradition going. During this process, I ate breakfast and drank some decaf coffee and lost track of time. Chart came into my room and asked me when I was going to take my shower, I replied that I was almost finished and we still had plenty of time.

After I read through the last obit, my spirit guide Stephanie came through to tell me some things about my two oldest sisters. All the information Stephanie gave me, only took two minutes (our time). I couldn't wait to talk to them, but I had to take Chart to his appointment first, then a hair appointment. Luckily, Chart didn't have to have the procedure after all, so after I dropped him at home, I headed to my hair appointment with Tracy at Market Place Mall, then drove over to Yvonne's to see if what Stephanie had told me was true. Stephanie had said that when Yvonne was around seven or eight years old, she had a special friend. Her special friend was light-skinned and looked similar to her. Yvonne had tried to tell Momma about this friend but was told that her friend was imaginary and she should not talk about it. This friend was with her for about four years. My guide also said that Yvonne's ability is being able to read pictures. Yvonne can look at a picture and tell if something is wrong with the person in it. She confirmed that this ability was true, but that she had never tried to fully develop it. It just comes naturally.

Next, I talked to Yvonne about a trip to South Carolina that she and Linda once took with Mom and Dad. My understanding is that some type of entity attached itself to Linda and was brought back home and she was constantly tormented by it. Then Linda had terrifying dreams about demons and started seeing them outside of her dreams. Momma had assumed Linda was having really bad nightmares and maybe it had something to do with what she was eating before she went to sleep. I can't imagine how Linda must have felt, all that fear, the aloneness, the confusion. Stephanie also told me that the entities Linda brought back from South Carolina were trying to keep her from dreaming because she is a prophetic dreamer and an astral traveler. (Whenever we talk, she tells me about some of her dreams.)

Stephanie also told me that at age 17, Linda had a psychotic break and had to be put on meds. Linda verified all of this. She is a strong person. Parents not believing their children when they talk about the paranormal is why I want to have a place for crystal and indigo children to go to be able to talk to people who understand what they are going through. Crystal children have an opalescent color aura and before the age of six or seven are showing signs of being highly sensitive or psychic and are very spiritual young children. Indigo children or young adults have an indigo or blue color aura and are older than seven years of age. Indigo children are also highly sensitive and many are clairvoyant. Because they are older it will be harder for them to hide their feelings and act as if everything is okay when they can sense that it's not.

Lastly, my guide said that we are the connection of three sisters (sounds like the *Charmed* sisters on TV). I must confess, there has always been a special bond between Yvonne, Linda and me. I used to think it was because I relate well to older people, but all this time, it has been because we are psychically connected. Poor Mom; I bet she was ready to pull out her hair when I came along and started taking about seeing dead people. Wow, three sensitive sisters in one family! I wasn't by myself, and that's why whenever I had talked to them about all the strange things I saw and experienced, they had been supportive and always made me feel like my ability was a gift, not a curse.

I left Yvonne's house a little before 8:30p.m. When I got home, I had to start writing about what had happened. The next day when I got up, I felt tired and heavy. As I walked to the kitchen to get my vitamin drink and water, a shadow went past me. I assumed it was the guest who had come with the home. He normally doesn't come into the kitchen; he seems to be attached to the dining room and guest bedroom (both of these have wood-paneled walls), and I haven't quite figured out who he is yet.

The day we first saw the house and I walked in to check it out, I could sense he was there, but the house had a special energy in it that attracted me to it, and I had to have it. Getting back to our house guest, after living in the house about a month I was finally able to see that he was in his twenties and white, I sensed he had been very ill, and had only been able to go from his bedroom to the dining area to eat. My readings are all done in the dining room because it is big and because of the strong energies that are present. The weird thing was that I had not felt his presence for months while writing this book. And I knew that the shadow that had just gone by me didn't feel like him.

Having this man in my house has never bothered me. He is sort of playful, as Yonna, Karen, and Myesha found out one day when they were at my house for a reading. I headed to my back room and sat down on the couch, and all hell broke loose. A bunch of different spirits were all in my head at the same time, talking and talking. *"Stop!"* I yelled. "I can't understand you, it's too many talking all at once." *Oh, no, what did I do?* I wondered. *Why are there so many? This has never happened before.* Getting overwhelmed, I got out my journal and started writing down what I could actually hear coming through, but I missed a lot because they were talking so fast. I prayed that these spirits wouldn't follow me when I left for work.

That same day, that all the spirits came through, I had an appointment with E, my therapist. The doctor at Primecare at Northpoint had thought speaking with a therapist would be a good start at assessing why I was continually having problems with insomnia. Everybody kept telling me to try meditation. I have been doing meditation for years, and it is a wonderfully relaxing and calming experience; my problem was that I could meditate in the morning with no problem, but meditating at night after picking up stuff about and off of associates and customers all day, was a challenge. It didn't matter how many times I cleared myself. Being a sensitive, I wasn't able to get it all out of my mind.

At my session with E later that afternoon, I told her about all of my uninvited guests. She said that I needed to tell them very firmly that they were invading my privacy and they needed to leave (easier said than done). E helped me a lot during our many sessions. At home and at work, I am the therapist. I feel I am a good listener and I give out good advice, plus it helps that I am able to sense things about people after being around them for a while, so it was a positive experience to have someone who would be honest with me and give me her professional opinion. E helped me to realize that I had too many projects going on at one time and that this was contributing to my restlessness at night. I was working a full-time job (40–45 hours a week), had been put in charge of fundraising for the Susan G Komen foundation then the United Way by myself from April to October (thank you, Frann, for all your help with great giveaways), was writing a book (that I worked on daily from four to six hours a day), was still doing readings for people, was doing Reiki on Mr. G once every two weeks or more if I was able, was going over to the hospital to see people who were sick and was doing 20-minute Reiki sessions at work to raise money. Lastly, a carnival that I had planned and organized for the month of July got cancelled at the last minute. I was ready for a break.

Getting back to my uninvited guests, I had received information from spirit guides for five co-workers. After leaving E's office, I went back to work and told two associates what I had received from their spirit guides. The rest of the day, I tried to stay away from people to get my head straight. When I arrived home after 10p.m., however, my guests were still there. I did what E had told me to do, telling them all to leave with a strong and demanding voice. I repeated this three times and felt some leave (probably the five guides/spirits I had gotten information from earlier in the day. Several still remained in the house.

I made it through Thursday, then Friday. This happened to be Tax Free Weekend, so we closed late. It was Friday, around 11:00p.m., by the time I got home, and I was exhausted. While I was in my room, changing into my sleep clothes, Chart came in and asked me who was in our house. Several nights before when I had told them to leave, I had woke him up but lied and told him that I was hollering at the dogs, but tonight, after he fell asleep, somebody had pulled his covers off him. Then Mokey, his cat (notice I said his), jumped from out of the closet and onto the bed to protect him. He said Mokey was swiping at something and making screeching sounds.

Now I felt really bad, but I was trying to keep my husband out of it. I didn't want to worry him, but I came clean and tried to explain what had been going on in our home since Wednesday. On Saturday morning, Chart went to the grocery store and I called Priest to tell him what was going on and to see if he or Anika (Priest's wife) would be going to the flea market that day, because I needed some white sage to smudge the house and myself (white sage is the strongest). While talking to Priest, I began to cry, but I have to admit, I didn't know if it was me actually crying or the empath in me picking up on an emotion in one of the spirits because they knew that I was going to do whatever it took to make them leave. Having those spirits there made me feel like I was carrying around a heavy bag of clothes on my back. It wasn't as if I felt that they were negative, but mostly, having more than one at a time to deal with overwhelms me; they all want me to hear them, so they can be quite pushy.

Priest asked if I was okay and if I needed him to come over, but I told him I was fine. Anika wasn't able to go to the flea market Saturday but did go on Sunday, and she couldn't find white sage but found sweet-grass.

That Sunday, I had to be at work by 1p.m., but I felt I needed to do something before I left. There were three white candles on my altar, so I put them in a triangle on the dining table and poured sea salt to connect them. As I lit each candle, I repeated, "Connection of three are the powers that be." I cleansed my quartz crystal and two purple sponges and laid the crystal at the top point of the triangle and a sponge on each side. My angel cards were on my altar, so I got them, sat down at the base of the triangle, and did an angel   reading on myself for guidance for the first time. The first card from the deck was for my past: "Chakra Clearing" (Archangel Metatron: call upon me to clear and open your chakras using sacred geometric shapes). I placed it to the left. The next card was for the present: "Clairvoyance" (Archangel Raziel: I am helping your spiritual sight to awaken fully so you can clearly see heavenly love). I placed it to the right. The last card, the future, was "Angel Therapy" (Archangel Raphael: give your cares and worries to us angels, and allow us to take your burdens). This last card, I put at the top of the triangle.

I stood there, just staring at the cards. Clairvoyance. Was I ready for this new ability? Obviously, I don't have a choice. I placed my crystal on the first card and asked that the spirits please move on and give me some time to adjust to what was happening to me. I repeated this for each of the other two cards. After about 30 minutes, amazingly, I was feeling lighter. More spirits had left, but two still lingered. They were female, but that was all I sensed. When it was time to leave for work, I felt much clearer.

Anika and Gabby dropped off the sweet-grass that afternoon. Anika is a very thoughtful daughter-in-law, and she has helped me out a lot recently. I love her dearly.

I had decided to wait until I was off Tuesday to do the smudging because I wanted to do it right and not rush it and couldn't do that on a day when I was working. At work, Princess, one of the young ladies I had given a message to from her guide a few days before, gave me the name of one of her dad's friends, who also has special abilities. Momma AZ (Arizona). I was working some long hours and didn't have time or energy for much of anything, but when I got home that Monday night, after speaking with another person and giving that person the message from a guide, I called Momma AZ. I told Arizona that I was Princess's friend from work. We started talking, and I told her about all of my visitors and what had been happening to me since the beginning of the year. She asked me to hold on while she did a three-way call to Princess. When Princess picked up, she asked what time it was, and I said 9:40p.m. Then I laughed, because I had called Momma AZ at 9:04p.m. and she had called Princess at 9:40p.m. Next, Arizona asked me what my date of birth was. I told her. She paused for a moment to add up the numbers and said it was no wonder I was getting a double whammy for increased abilities because this is the Age of Aquarius and I am a #5 (birth-date numerology).In numerology, all digits dropping the 9s have to be added together to get a single number: 2+1+5+1+5=14:1+4=5.) Momma AZ told me to embrace these new abilities because they are another gift and will come at me fast and strong. The date of the phone call (8/1/2012) was also relevant: 8+1+2+1+2=14(1+4=5).

After I got off the phone, I started really focusing on the number five. My address has 5's in it, and so did my old address. Five spirits came through to me. I am the fifth child in the family. I did my first connection-of-three clearing on the fifth day of the month, I was married on the 14th (1+4=5). Wow! How crazy is that? I finally fell off to sleep around midnight. I woke up to go to the bathroom and looked at the clock; it was 5:05a.m. After lying back down and falling back off to sleep, I woke up again at 7:55a.m. After all that, I knew that the coming Tuesday would be a good day to smudge myself and my home.

Wednesday morning was a bright and beautiful day, and all my guests were gone. Next time, I hope they remember to come back to me one at a time, and I will be glad to help them in any way I can.

My family from left, John, Chris, Michelle, Darrin and Tomorris

Back row: Yvonne, Millie and Linda.
Front row: Robbin, Michelle, Darrin and Jackie
(Darrin and Michelle's wedding)

Celebrating our 30th anniversary, from left,
Chart, Robbin, Pilar, Priest and Gabby

Robbin Campbell grew up in Winston-Salem, North Carolina. She is 54 years old and had her first interaction with the spirit world at the age of six. She has been married for 38 years to her husband, Surachart. They have two children, Priest and Pilar; four grandchildren, Daisean, Gabrielle, Jermelle Jr., and Jaiel; one great-grandchild, Tristan; a daughter-in-law, Anika; and a son-in-law, Jermelle.

Robbin has worked in retail management for the past 32 years, 14 at Davis Department Store and the past 18 at Belk. Being a sensitive, she has also had the privilege for the past 15 years to do readings for hundreds of clients, and by doing Reiki, she has helped with healing, relaxation, and medical diagnosis for both family and friends. Her husband is from Thailand, so the family has had the opportunity to travel there many times. She feels lucky to have this special gift.

CPSIA information can be obtained at www.ICGtesting.com
Printed in the USA
BVOW05s0150170314

347785BV00006B/10/P